FOR YOUR INFORMATION 3

HIGH-INTERMEDIATE READING SKILLS

FYi

Karen Blanchard ♦ Christine Root

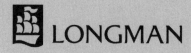

LONGMAN

For Your Information 3

Pearson Education, 10 Bank Street, White Plains, NY 10606

Editorial Director: Joanne Dresner
Senior Acquisitions Editor: Allen Ascher
Development Editor: Françoise Leffler
Production Editor: Christine Cervoni
Photo Research: Amy Durfy
Text Composition: Naomi Ganor, Kathleen Marks, Kim Teixeira
Text Design: Taurins Design Associates
Cover Design: Taurins Design Associates
Text Art: Yoshi Miyake 8, 43, 80, 98, 146, 204; Sarah Sloane 38, 120, 134, 152, 161, 209.

Grateful acknowledgment is given to the following for providing photographs:
p.11, Globe Photo/Richard Carpenter; p.17, Stock Boston © David Simson; p.28, Allsport/Mike Powell; p.30, Al Messerschmidt © NBA Photos; p.46, International Stock Photo © Bill O'Connor/ Daily Telegraph Colour Library; p.52, © Jane Scherr/Jeroboam, Inc.; p.64, © 1996 Estate of Pablo Picasso/Artists Rights Society (ARS), New York; p.68, Archive Photos/Express Newspapers; pp.70–71, Isabella Stewart Gardner Museum, Boston; p.73, Reuters/HO/Archive Photos; p.82, FPG International © Telegraph Colour Library; p.91, March of Dimes Birth Defects Foundation; p.93, Liaison International © Spencer Grant; p.113, The Image Bank © Mieke Maas; p.124, Barry Chin/The Boston Globe; p.172, Liaison International © J. Wilson; p.179, FPG International © Larry Mulvehill; p.194, General Motors Corporation; p.198 (top), Esprit; p.198 (bottom), Photographer Darren Keith; p.211, Stock Boston © Michael Dwyer; p.218, © 1996 Capital Cities/ABC, Inc.

Text credits appear on page 232.

Library of Congress Cataloging-in-Publication Data

Blanchard, Karen Lourie, 1951-
    For your information 3: high-intermediate reading skills / Karen Blanchard,
Christine Root.
        p. cm.
    ISBN 0-201-87798-8
    1. English language—Textbooks for foreign speakers. 2. Readers.
I. Root, Christine Baker, 1945- . II. Title.
PE1128.B5862 1996
428.6'4—dc20   96-19323
                                                       CIP

        6 7 8 9 10-CRS-01

To David,
in grateful recognition
of his manifold contributions
to so many aspects of
For Your Information 1, 2, and *3.*

CONTENTS

For Your Information 3 is a book of authentic, pre-academic readings for high-intermediate students of English as a Second Language. It is a reading skill-builder designed to appeal to students who are ready to take on the challenges of reading "uncontrolled" language from mainstream sources. It is meant for use in adult education programs, universities, language institutes, and secondary schools in both the United States and abroad.

Like *FYI 1* and *FYI 2*, *FYI 3* is made up of eight thematically based units, each of which contains a selection of three or four articles, stories, poems, essays, or interviews. It is based on research indicating that ESL students are able to read at a higher level of English than they can produce. Provocative discussion questions and relevant skill-building activities accompany each unit as a whole and each individual reading.

It is the intention of *FYI 3* to help students become increasingly less tied to text and more adept at the application and analysis of information from their reading and the thoughtful discussion of ideas. While it is fundamentally a reading text, *FYI 3* also calls on students to practice their speaking, listening, writing, and analytical skills.

The basic format for each unit in *FYI 3* is as follows:

- **Points to Ponder**
  Thought-provoking prereading questions introduce the general topic of each unit and generate discussion and interest in the topic.

- **Reading Selections and Tasks**
  Each unit contains three to four authentic reading selections on high-interest topics of universal appeal. Selections are followed by a combination of discussion questions and activities to help students
    - expand their vocabulary by using context to figure out meaning, understand idioms, and define terms and by studying and using word forms;
    - hone their reading skills through a variety of strategies such as previewing, predicting, skimming, scanning, recognizing main ideas, looking at style, separating fact from theory, and understanding point of view;
    - gain experience with exercises that replicate those on the TOEFL exam;
    - develop their writing skills by summarizing, paraphrasing, and applying information in short reports.

● **Tying It All Together**
Each unit concludes with a set of questions that encourage students to think about, distill, and discuss the ideas they have read about in the unit. Following the questions are an activity that is included *Just for Fun* and a *Reader's Journal* in which students are asked to reflect, in writing, on the ideas and information in each unit.

We hope that you and your students enjoy working through the readings and activities in this text and that you find the text interesting *for your information*.

KLB, CBR

ACKNOWLEDGMENTS

As always, we would like to thank our families, friends, and editors for their forbearance as we worked our way through this series. Special thanks go to Hasan Halkali for his high standards in determining which articles to include and to our editor, Allen Ascher, for his discerning suggestions.

STRIVING TO COMMUNICATE

FYi

Unit·1

Selections

Throughout the world, wherever there is human society, there is language. Language is the form of communication characterized by the use of spoken or written symbols with agreed-upon meanings. It is only because we can communicate with each other that we have been able to develop civilizations. Advances in science, technology, economics, art, literature, and government are all the results of people communicating.

Think about and then discuss the following questions.

1. All human societies have developed some form of language. What other systems of communication can you think of besides language?

   _____

   _____

2. The exact origins of language remain a mystery. Although there are many theories, none of them has been proven. How do you think language developed? Do you have any theories?

3. How many languages do you know? What other languages do you wish you could speak? Why?

4. How do you think children learn their native languages? In what ways do you think learning a second language is similar to or different from learning a first language?

B. C. by Johnny Hart

By permission of Johnny Hart and Creators Syndicate, Inc.

Although our world is growing smaller through international trade, telecommunications, and transportation, people still have difficulty communicating with each other. Thousands of languages are spoken around the world today. Some people think that the answer to the problems in global communication is the use of an artificial international language. In **The Hope of Esperanto,** you will read about one such language, called Esperanto, which was developed in 1887 by Ludovic Zamenhof and is still in use today.

BEFORE YOU READ

PREREADING QUESTIONS

1. Would you be interested in learning an artificial language such as Esperanto?

2. What are the advantages and disadvantages of such a language?

The Hope of Esperanto
(La Espero de Esperanto)

BY J.D. REED

REPORTED BY EDWARD M. GOMEZ/NEW YORK AND PAUL HOFHEINZ/LONDON

A made-up tongue celebrates its centenary

1 In 1887 Ludovic Zamenhof, a multilingual Polish oculist, published a book introducing a new language under the pseudonym Dr. Esperanto, meaning "one who hopes." Zamenhof fervently wished that his invented tongue would become the world's second language. Although that hope is

Kreita lingvo festas sian centjariĝon

1 En 1887 Ludoviko Zamenhof, multlingva pola okulisto, publikigis libron prezentantan novan lingvon sub la kaŝnomo Doktoro Esperanto. Zamenhof arde deziris ke lia inventita lingvo fariĝu la dua lingvo de la mondo. Kvankam tiu espero estas ankoraŭ nerealigita,

still unrealized, nearly 6,000 zealous Esperantists—the largest gathering ever—from as far away as Japan and Brazil are in Warsaw this week to honor Zamenhof on the occasion of the 100th birthday of his language. They are doing so with a variety of events, all in Esperanto, plus a visit to Zamenhof's hometown of Bialystok.

2   Many people assume that Esperanto is a dying language, a verbal experiment that has simply not worked out. In fact, Esperantists can be found all around the world. Estimates of their total number vary widely, from 1 million to 8 million or more. Marjorie Duncan, 65, a retired Sydney, Australian schoolteacher, believes the movement needs more young people. But, she says, they would "rather drive cars or go surfing."

3   At a glance, Esperanto seems simple enough. It has only 16 easily memorized rules of grammar—no exceptions—and a basic vocabulary built from mostly Indo-European roots. Experts claim that virtually anyone can learn Esperanto in 100 hours or less. But for some, numerous suffixes and prefixes may complicate matters. Accents always fall on the next-to-last syllable of a word. (*J* sounds like *y*, *ĉ* like *ch*, *ĝ* like *j*, *ŝ* like *sh* and *u* like *oo*.) The no-frills system can

preskaŭ sesmil fervoraj esperantistoj—historie la plej granda renkontiĝo—tiel foraj lokoj kiel Japanio kaj Brazilo estas ĉi-semajne en Varsovio por honori Zamenhof je la okazo de la centa datreveno de lia lingvo. Ili celbras per diversaj aranĝoj, ĉiuj en Esperanto, plus vizito al la hejmurbo de Zamenhof, Bjalistoko.

2   Multaj homoj supozas, ke Esperanto estas unu mortanta lingvo, vorta eksperimento kiu simple ne elsukcesis. Fakte, esperantistoj estas troveblaj tra la tuta mondo. Taksoj pri ilia tuta nombro multe varias, inter 1 milionoj kaj 8 milionoj aŭ pli. Marjorie Duncan, 65-jara, emerita instruistino el Sidneo, Aŭstralio, kredas, ke la movado bezonas pli da gejunuloj. Sed, ŝi diras, ili preferus "veturigi aŭtojn aŭ iri surfumi."

3   Je unua rigardo, Esperanto ŝajnas sufiĉe simpla. La lingvo havas nur 16 facile memoreblajn gramatikajn regulojn—sen iuj ajn esceptoj—kaj bazan vortaron konstruitan el plejparte hindeŭropaj radikoj. Fakuloj pretendas, ke preskaŭ iu ajn persono povas lerni Esperanton en cent horoj aŭ malpli. Sed ĉe keikaj homoj, multnombraj sufiksoj kaj prefiksoj eble komplikos aferojn. La senornama sistemo ankaŭ kapablas trakti muitajn idiotismajn frazerojn el aliaj lingvoj kaj ja havassiajn proprajn

handle many idiomatic phrases from other languages, and even has its own earthy expletives, such as *diable* for hell and *merdo* for excrement.

4 The use of Esperanto probably reached its peak in the 1920s, when idealists embraced it as one small step toward peace. Some intellectuals viewed it as a solution to the language problem, which they felt contributed to political misunderstandings; in some British schools youngsters could study Esperanto. But interest died down after World War II, partly because governments did not support the language, partly because English was fast becoming the lingua franca of business and travel. Esperantists have urged the United Nations to adopt their language, but the organization has its hands full with six officials ones (English, French, Spanish, Arabic, Chinese and Russian).

5 Humphrey Tonkin, president of the Rotterdam-based Universal Esperanto Association, says the *Lingvo Internacia* is popular in lands whose languages do not travel well. Examples: Iran, Brazil, the Netherlands and the Scandinavian countries. A sizable concentration of Esperantists is found in Japan, where the language has sometimes been used for discussions by scientists who speak different languages. China uses Esperanto to facilitate communication between speakers of its northern and southern dialects and supports an active publishing program. Many masterpieces of literature have been translated into Esperanto, including the Koran and some of Shakespeare's plays. But Mary Davies, an Esperantist who runs a hotel in Heysham, England, complains, "We don't have any light reading."

6 When they travel, many Esperantists wear lapel pins shaped like green stars that signal them as Esperanto speakers,

sukoplenajn sakraĵojn, kiel ekzemple diable kaj merdo.

4 La uzo de Esperanto eble atingis sian pinton en la 20aj jaroj, kiam idealistoj alpropriĝis ĝin kiel unu etan paŝon al paco. Kelkaj intelektuloj rigardis ĝin kiel solvon al tiu lingva problemo kiu, laŭ ili, kontribuas al politikaj miskomprenoj; en kelkaj britaj lernejoj, gejunuloj povis studi Esperanton. Sed la intereso malfortiĝis post la Dua Mondmilito parte ĉar regisaroj ne subtenis la lingvon kaj ankaŭ parte ĉar la angla rapide fariĝis la komuna lingvo de komerco kaj vojaĝado. Esperantistoj instigis Unuiĝintajn Naciojn adopti ilian lingvon, sed la organizaĵo jam havas plenajn manojn pro ses oficialaj lingvoj (angla, franca, hispana, araba, ĉina kaj rusa).

5 Humphrey Tonkin, prezidanto de la Universala Esperanto-Asocio en Roterdamo, diras, ke la Lingvo Internacia estas populara en landoj kies lingvoj ne bone vojaĝas. Ekzemple: Irano, Brazilo, Nederlando kaj la skandinavaj landoj. Konsiderinda koncentriĝo de esperantistoj ankaŭ troveblas en Japanio, kie la lingvo estis foje uzata por diskutoj inter scientistoj, kiuj parolas malsamajn naciajn lingvojn. Ĉinio uzas Esperanton por faciligi komunikadon inter parolantoj de siaj nordaj kaj sudaj dialektoj kaj subtenas aktivan eldonprogramon. Multajn literaturajn ĉefverkojn oni tradukis en Esperanton, inkluzive la Koranon kaj kelkajn teatraĵojn de Sekspiro. Sed Mary Davies, esperantistino kiu estras hotelon en Heysham, Anglio, plendas, "Ni ne havas ian leĝeran legaĵon."

6 Kiam ili vojaĝas, multaj esperantistoj portas insignojn en formo de verdaj steloj por indiki sian esperantistecon, esperante renkonti samlingvanojn. Ili ankaŭ telefonas al kunkonversaciantoj

in the hope of meeting fellow speakers. They also call up comrades-in-conversation and exchange cassette tapes by mail. Says Scotsman William Auld: "I've gotten drunk in every country in Europe with Esperanto speakers." In any language, an avid conversationalist can work up quite a thirst for a wee drop of *viskio*.

kaj interŝanĝas kasedojn perpoŝte. Diras skoto William Auld: "Mi ebriiĝis en ĉiu lando de Eŭropo kun Esperanto-parolantoj." En ĉiu ajn lingvo, avida konversacianto povas elfacriki imponan soifon je eta guteto de viskio.

● ●

HOW WELL DID YOU READ?

Read the following statements. If a statement is true, write *T* on the line. If it is false, write *F*.

_____ 1. Esperanto has become the world's second language.

_____ 2. Esperanto is a dying language.

_____ 3. The total number of Esperantists is 8 million.

_____ 4. Everyone agrees that Esperanto is a simple language to learn.

_____ 5. The use of Esperanto has decreased since the 1920s.

_____ 6. Esperanto is used to make communication easier between people who do not speak the same language.

_____ 7. Many literary masterpieces can be read in Esperanto.

BUILDING READING SKILLS

LOCATING INFORMATION

Look in the article for answers to the following questions. Underline the sentences that give you the information you need in order to answer each question. Then write the number of the question next to the sentences you underlined.

1. Why does Esperanto seem simple to learn?

2. Why was Esperanto most popular in the 1920s?

3. Why did interest in Esperanto decrease after World War II?

4. Why is Esperanto popular in Iran, Brazil, the Netherlands, and the Scandinavian countries?

5. How do Esperantists keep in touch with each other?

Find a synonym for each of the following words or expressions from the article. The number of the paragraph is given to help you.

1. language (¶1) _____

2. enthusiastic (¶1) _____

3. just (¶2) _____

4. differ (¶2) _____

5. many (¶3) _____

6. manage (¶3) _____

7. basic (¶3) _____

8. encouraged (¶4) _____

9. countries (¶5) _____

10. aid (¶5) _____

Every known language includes the *a* sound as in the English word *father*.

Encyclopedias are a good place to look up basic information on a subject. You can find encyclopedias in almost every library. Encyclopedias are also available for use on computers. The following article about **Esperanto** is from the *Academic American Encyclopedia,* which is a computer-based reference. Read the article to see what additional information you can find out about Esperanto.

● ●

ESPERANTO

BY FRANKLIN E. HOROWITZ

1 Esperanto is an artificial language designed to serve internationally as an auxiliary means of communication among speakers of different languages. The creation of Ludovic Lazar Zamenhof, a Polish-Jewish ophthalmologist, Esperanto was first presented in 1887. An international movement to promote its use, although originally plagued with dissension, has continued to flourish and has members in more than 80 countries.

2 Esperanto is used internationally across language boundaries by at least one million people, particularly in specialized fields. It is used in personal contacts, on radio broadcasts, and in a number of publications as well as in translations of both modern works and classics. Its popularity has spread from Europe—both East and West—to such countries as Brazil and Japan. It is, however, in China that Esperanto had had its greatest impact. It is taught in universities and used in many translations (often in scientific or technological works). *El Popola Cînio (From People's China),* a monthly magazine in Esperanto, is read worldwide. Radio Beijing's Esperanto program is the most popular program in Esperanto in the world.

3 Esperanto's vocabulary is drawn primarily from Latin, the Romance languages, English, and German. Spelling is completely regular. A simple and consistent set of endings indicates grammatical functions of words. Thus, for example, every noun ends in *o,* every adjective in *a,* and the infinitive

of every verb in *i*. Esperanto also has a highly productive system of constructing new words from old: *ami*, to love; *malami*, to hate; *malamemo*, the tendency to hate.

Bibliography: Foster, Peter G., *The Esperanto Movement* (1982); Goodman, Thomas H., *Elements of Esperanto* (1977); Pei, Mario, *One Language for the World* (1958); Richardson, D., *Esperanto* (1988).

● ●

Make a list of three new things you learned about Esperanto from the encyclopedia article.

1. _____

2. _____

3. _____

TALK IT OVER

DISCUSSION QUESTIONS

1. Do you think the idea of an invented universal language is a good one? What would it be useful for? What problems might it solve? What problems might it cause?

2. Do you think the people of your country could accept the idea of a universal language? Why or why not?

BUILDING WRITING SKILLS

APPLICATION OF INFORMATION

From what you have read about Esperanto, do you think it would be an easy or a difficult language to learn? In small groups, use your knowledge of English, your native language, and information from the articles to translate this Esperanto paragraph into English.

La inteligenta persono lernas la interlingvon Esperanto rapide kai facile. Esperanto estas la moderna kultura lingvo por la internacia mondo. Simpla, fleksebla, praktiva solvo de la problemo de universala interkompreno, Esperanto meritas vian seriozan konsideron. Lernu la interlingvon Esperanto.[1]

_____

_____

_____

_____

_____

_____

Read the following selection as quickly as possible and decide which title is the most appropriate. Write the title on the line.

1. How to Communicate in Sign Language

2. Sign Language: A Clue to the Origins of Language

3. The Origin of Speech

4. Sign Languages around the World

Sign language is a method of communication that relies on hand movements and other gestures. It is a language used successfully with many people who are deaf and hearing-impaired. But sign language is probably nothing new. The work of paleoanthropologists, the scientists who study primitive humanlike creatures, has shown that the origin of language may lie in gestures, not speech as had previously been assumed. Until relatively recently, it was universally believed that the word "language" referred only to speech. It was also believed that language emerged suddenly in our species and that language was a learned, not an innate, behavior. As scientists learn more and more about our ancient ancestors and the processes of the brain, attitudes are changing. They are beginning to understand that sign language is not primitive. It is linguistically as complex as speech. In fact, deaf children all over the world learn sign language just as hearing children learn speech because signing and speech both draw on many of the same parts of the brain.[2]

Su-Kyeong Kim came to the United States from Korea at the age of fifteen knowing almost no English. She went to a private high school near Boston, and within four years succeeded not only in learning English, but also in writing a book about her experiences as an international student. In this newspaper article, **Reaping the Rewards of Learning English,** you will read about some of those experiences.

BEFORE YOU READ

PREREADING ACTIVITY

Which of the following skills have been the most difficult for you in learning English? Which have been the easiest? Rank each item, with 1 being the easiest, and then compare your ratings with those of your classmates.

_____ pronunciation

_____ grammar

_____ vocabulary

_____ writing

_____ reading

_____ speaking

_____ listening

_____ idioms and slang

_____ gestures

_____ (other) _____

Su-Kyeong Kim

Reaping the Rewards of Learning English

By Jean Caldwell

1   At Sunday's graduation, Su-Kyeong Kim will speak to the 385 members of her class at Northfield Mount Hermon School. This might seem an amazing feat for a girl who spoke hardly a word of English when she came here from Korea four years ago at age 15.

2   But Kim herself is amazing. Besides becoming so fluent in English that she hasn't even a trace of an accent, Kim also has won numerous academic

awards and has written a book about her experiences struggling with the language. Her teachers hope she will find a publisher soon for "Looking for Trouble," her 147-page, hand-bound volume.

3   Kim saw the need for the book when she began helping newly arrived Korean students at the school and realized the newcomers suffered the same qualms she had.

4   "You think you are the only person being embarrassed, humiliated, making mistakes," she said in a recent interview on campus. "But everyone does it."

OK to Make Mistakes

5   She calls her book "Looking for Trouble" to signify that the road leading to success in mastering a second language is a risky path. "I want others to know that it's OK to make mistakes," she said, "that nothing worthwhile is without risk."

6   "Lots of people think other people do not make a lot of mistakes or are not as embarrassed as they are. It's not true. Everyone is embarrassed when they make a mistake and everyone makes mistakes. You can turn that mistake into a greater step to your success."

7   The book evolved from a series of papers she wrote for her junior English class describing her experiences as a newcomer to this country.

8   She wrote about what she called her "hellish arrival" in the United States when she and her mother shuttled frantically back and forth between the airports in New York City because of bad advice. She described their fear on a midnight taxi ride from Boston to Northfield because they could not understand the explanation given by their driver, long-haired and wearing torn jeans, as he stopped in a dimly lit parking lot near a long, dark building.

Innocent Misunderstandings

9   She wrote of her encounter with a teacher who was aghast when she mispronounced the word "sheet" in asking for a piece of paper and her bewildered dismay when her enthusiastic "Yes!" caused a student who had asked to sit at her lunch table to turn away. A friend told her the other girl had asked, "Do you mind if I sit with you?" Su-Kyeong had heard, "May I sit with you?"

10   Her advice to those studying a second language: "Look for trouble. Be gutsy. Be daring. You have to dare to learn another language. You can't sit in your own room and analyze grammar. You have to go and talk to people and listen to them."

11   In addition to the book and being chosen class orator at graduation, Kim's rewards for following her own advice were winning the English as a Second Language Award in the spring of her freshman year, the Junior Class English Prize and the Departmental Award for Chinese 2. She also is a member of the Cum Laude Society.

12   In September, Su-Kyeong will enter Stanford University in California where she plans to study Japanese and international business.

QUOTES FROM "Looking for Trouble"

"One of the hardest things for a foreigner is the feeling of being constantly left out—not deliberately, but by the inadequacy of one's own knowledge of language and culture. Because we want to feel part of the group, we are always watching others' faces to see how the wind blows."

"I started excluding reading when people asked me about my hobbies. No more lying on the bed with my feet on the wall. You can't use 10 highlighters and a thick dictionary while you are flat on your back. Instead, I sat up straight and rigid in a hard chair, trying to burn as much new vocabulary and as many fresh idioms into my brain as possible. Sometimes I had to use my dictionary 30 times just to get a rough picture of what was going on."

HOW WELL DID YOU READ?

Write the answers to the following questions.

1. Why does the author call Kim amazing?

   _____

   _____

2. When did Kim realize that there was a need for a book about her experiences in learning English?

   _____

   _____

3. Why did she decide to call her book "Looking for Trouble"?

   _____

   _____

4. What are some things Kim wrote about in her book?

   _____

   _____

5. What advice does Kim give to people who are studying a second language?

   _____

   _____

TALK IT OVER

DISCUSSION
QUESTIONS

1. Do you agree with Kim's advice about learning a new language? Why or why not?

2. If you were writing a book like Kim's, what would the focus of your book be? What kinds of things would you write about? What advice would you give to others learning a second language? What would the title of your book be?

3. Would you be interested in reading Kim's book? Why or why not?

4. How would you describe Kim? What kind of a person do you think she is?

5. Read the quotes from "Looking for Trouble" and discuss them with your classmates.

EXPANDING VOCABULARY

A. Read each of the following sentences from the article. Then circle the letter of the choice that is closest in meaning to the highlighted phrase.

1. *This might seem **an amazing feat** for a girl who **spoke hardly a word of English** when she came here from Korea four years ago at age 15.*

   a. a small thing
   b. a remarkable accomplishment
   c. a big mistake

   a. knew almost no English
   b. was fluent in English
   c. spoke many words in English

2. ***Besides becoming so fluent in English** that **she hasn't even a trace of an accent**, Kim also has won numerous academic awards and has written a book about her experiences . . .*

   a. In addition to becoming so fluent in English
   b. Because she has become so fluent in English
   c. In spite of becoming so fluent in English

   a. she has a strong accent
   b. she doesn't have any accent
   c. she has a slight accent

3. *Kim saw the need for the book when she began helping newly arrived Korean students at the school and realized **the newcomers suffered the same qualms she had.***

   a. the new students were suffering more than she had
   b. she felt more secure than the newcomers
   c. the new students had the same feelings of uncertainty that she had

4. *The road leading to success in mastering a second language is **a risky path.***

    a. a dangerous road
    b. an easy trip
    c. a smooth step

5. *The book **evolved from a series of papers** she wrote for her junior English class describing her experiences as a newcomer to this country.*

    a. was written after she read the paper
    b. describes some articles
    c. developed out of some essays

B. **Cross out the word in each group that does not belong.**

1. aghast	shocked	exhausted	astonished
2. amazing	remarkable	extraordinary	routine
3. bewildered	wild	confused	perplexed
4. daring	gutsy	hesitant	brave
5. humiliated	delighted	embarrassed	ashamed

PROVERBS

Read and discuss the following sayings about language. Think of some more to add to the list.

1. Sticks and stones can break my bones, but words will never hurt me.

2. The pen is mightier than the sword.

3. If you can't say something nice, don't say anything at all.

4. Talk is cheap.

5. Actions speak louder than words.

Many of the world's thousands of languages may soon disappear. As technology improves, people around the world are relying more and more on electronic devices to communicate with each other. While this trend is helping the major languages, it is having a harmful effect on the minor ones. In the following newspaper article, **Half of World's Languages in Danger of Extinction,** you will read about the effects that advances in tele-communication are having on languages.

1. Do you know of any languages in your country that are dying out? Is anything being done to preserve them?

2. How do you think advances in technology might contribute to the death of certain languages?

3. Do any of your relatives speak a language that you cannot understand? Would you like to learn that language? Why or why not?

Half of World's Languages in Danger of Extinction

AS TECHNOLOGY LETS PEOPLE COMMUNICATE MORE, MAJOR LANGUAGES ARE STRENGTHENED AND MINOR ONES WEAKENED.

BY DANIEL Q. HANEY

1   ATLANTA—The world's 6,000 languages are dying off quickly, and up to half of them will probably become extinct during the next century, experts said yesterday.

2   "I call this a catastrophe—the rate of loss of mankind's linguistic diversity," said Michael Krauss of the University of Alaska.

3   While once languages were suppressed by government policy, the forces conspiring against native tongues now seem to be largely

electronic. Satellite television, cellular telephones, the Internet all let people speak to each other instantly all over the world, and all drive the need for languages that many understand.

4   In most cases, that language is English. Even defenders of dying languages concede that is not necessarily a bad thing, since a common language clearly allows people to communicate easily. For instance, scientists the world over often speak to each other in English, whether their labs are in France or Taiwan.

5   However, linguists at a conference yesterday of the American Association for the Advancement of Science urged the preservation of small languages as second, or even third, languages, rather than allowing them to be swallowed up by English, Arabic, Spanish and other major languages.

6   "We should care about this," Krauss said. "The world will be less interesting, less beautiful."

7   Krauss said that in prehistoric times, humans probably spoke 10,000 to 15,000 languages. This is now down to about 6,000 and dropping fast.

8   Krauss, who documents native Alaskan languages, estimated that between 20 percent and 50 percent of the world's languages were no longer being learned by children.

9   "They are beyond endangerment," he said. "They are the living dead," and will disappear in the next century.

10   The average language is spoken by 5,000 to 10,000 people. However, Krauss said that only those with more than one million speakers have a good future.

APOTHEKE

PHARMACY

PHARMACIE

GYÓGYSZERTÁR

FARMACIA

LJEKARNA

FARMACIA

ECZANE

ΦΑΡΜΑΚΕΙΟΝ

صيدلية

11   He estimated that about 600 of the world's languages are assured of still being around in 2100.

12   Many of the small languages on the verge of dying out are in tropical parts of the world, especially Africa and Indonesia, he said.

13   But the United States is also losing languages fast, especially in California, which has been called the world's third-most linguistically diverse region, after New Guinea and the Caucasus.

14   Leanne Hinton of the University of California at Berkeley said North America has 200 to 250 native languages, and about 50 of them are in California.

15   All the California Indian languages are in trouble. None is being learned widely by children or used in daily commerce. Twenty have died this century. The latest extinction occurred last month with the death of the lone speaker of Northern Pomo, a woman in her 80s.

16   Hinton said Native American languages were suppressed until the 1960s. Indian children sent to boarding schools were punished for speaking their parents' language.

17   Now, she said, a movement exists among California Indians to learn the elders' tongue before it's too late. Some tribes have set up summer language camps for youngsters.

18   "Despite the desires of the language activists, the outlook is somewhat grim," Hinton said. "There is no chance any of these will be first languages. But those who are trying to keep them alive are determined they will at least have a future as second languages."

19   Krauss doubts many new languages will be born. Latin, for instance, took 2,000 years to evolve into a dozen or so different European languages.

20   "Everybody, including bedouins on camels, will have wristwatch telephones," he said. "It is unlikely that Arabic will rediversify the way Latin did."

● ●

BUILDING READING SKILLS

RECOGNIZING MAIN IDEAS

Which of the following topics are discussed in the article? Put a check mark next to those topics.

_____ 1. the reasons some languages are becoming extinct

_____ 2. examples of languages that are in danger of dying out

_____ 3. how new languages will be born in the future

_____ 4. the need for languages that many people can understand

_____ 5. Native American languages

_____ 6. how cellular phones, satellite television, and the Internet work

HOW WELL DID YOU READ?

A. Read the following statements. If a statement is true, write _T_ on the line. If it is false, write _F_.

_____ 1. Scientists around the world often communicate in English.

_____ 2. Fewer languages were spoken in prehistoric times than are spoken today.

_____ 3. Only those languages with at least one million speakers will probably survive.

_____ 4. Most of the California Indian languages have a good chance of survival.

_____ 5. New languages are being born all the time.

_____ 6. Arabic has a good chance of rediversifying in the future.

_____ 7. The United States is one of the few places in the world that is not losing languages.

B. Circle the letter of the choice that best completes the sentence or answers the question.

1. The article mainly discusses _____ .

   a. the extinction of North American native languages
   b. how technology is strengthening major languages and weakening minor languages
   c. the similarities and differences between prehistoric and modern languages
   d. successful ways to keep minor languages alive

2. According to the author, which languages have a good chance of staying alive?

   a. those with 5,000 to 10,000 speakers
   b. Native American languages
   c. Alaskan languages
   d. those with over a million speakers

3. In which paragraph does the author mention some of the positive aspects of a common language?

   a. paragraph 3
   b. paragraph 4
   c. paragraph 5
   d. paragraph 7

4. The word *catastrophe* in paragraph 2 is closest in meaning to _____ .

   a. defense
   b. movement
   c. necessity
   d. disaster

5. The word *concede* in paragraph 4 is closest in meaning to _____ .

   a. admit
   b. disagree
   c. estimate
   d. communicate

(continued on the next page)

6. It can be inferred from the article that _____ .

   a. new languages are being born that will replace dying languages
   b. government policies about native languages are less suppressive now than they were in the past
   c. the world's major languages will probably rediversify in the future
   d. a common language has relatively little value in today's world

7. According to the article, which of the following is true of California Indian languages?

   a. None has died recently.
   b. Some are used in daily commerce.
   c. None is being learned widely by children.
   d. Some are in danger of extinction.

8. According to the author, how many years did it take for Latin to evolve into the major European languages?

   a. 6,000
   b. 2,000
   c. 5,000
   d. 600

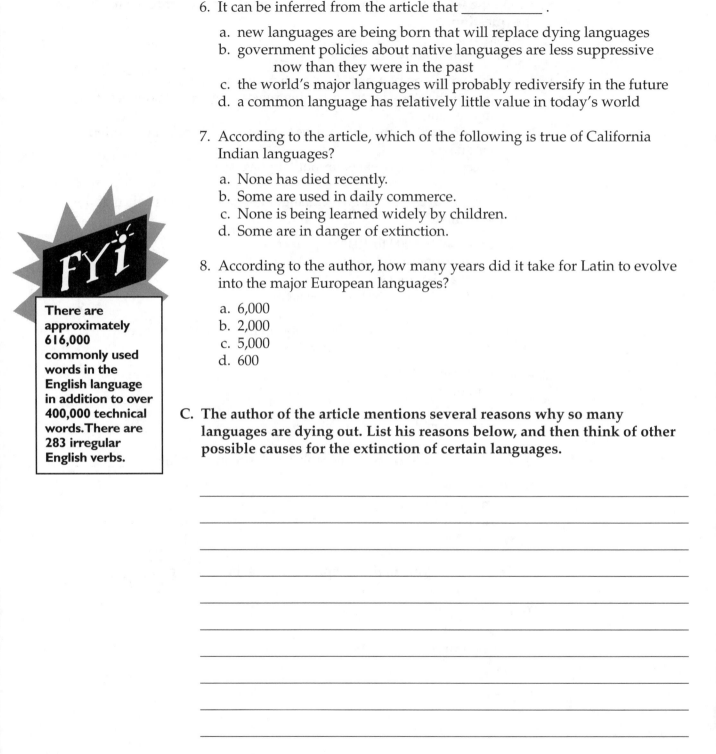

FYI

There are approximately 616,000 commonly used words in the English language in addition to over 400,000 technical words. There are 283 irregular English verbs.

C. **The author of the article mentions several reasons why so many languages are dying out. List his reasons below, and then think of other possible causes for the extinction of certain languages.**

_____

_____

_____

_____

_____

_____

_____

_____

_____

_____

BUILDING WRITING SKILLS

SUMMARIZING

Summarizing an article is a good way to help you understand the article and identify the author's main ideas. When you summarize, you should reduce the article to its main points in a few clear, concise sentences. Use the five "w"s (who, what, when, where, and why) to help you get started.

Here is a short paragraph that summarizes the article, "Reaping the Rewards of Learning English," from page 11.

Su-Kyeong Kim came to the United States when she was 15 years old, knowing almost no English. In addition to winning numerous academic awards and receiving an acceptance to Stanford University, Kim has also written a book about her experiences as a nonnative speaker of English. She wants other people in her position to know that it is all right to make mistakes and that it is important to take risks.

Use the space below to write a few sentences that summarize the main idea of "Half of World's Languages in Danger of Extinction."

_____

_____

_____

_____

TALK IT OVER

DISCUSSION QUESTIONS

1. How do you feel about the fact that some languages are dying out? Do you think languages represent culture and history? Read and discuss the following quotes on these subjects.

   a. "I am always sorry when any language is lost because languages are the pedigree of nations." (Samuel Johnson)

   b. "Language is the archive of history." (Ralph Waldo Emerson)

   c. "There is no such thing as an ugly language. Today I hear every language as if it were the only one, and when I hear of one that is dying, it overwhelms me as though it were the death of the earth." (Elias Canetti)[3]

   d. "To rescue from oblivion even a fragment of a language which men have used and which is in danger of being lost . . . is to extend the scope of social observation and to serve civilization." (Victor Hugo)

2. Besides languages, what can you think of that is dying out as the world becomes "smaller" and more technological?

3. How do you think minor languages can be kept alive?

WORD FORMS Many English words have verb, noun, adjective, and adverb forms. Knowing the meanings of the words and how to use the different forms will expand your vocabulary and improve your reading skills. Study the following chart of words that appeared in this unit.

VERB	NOUN	ADJECTIVE	ADVERB
argue	argument	arguable argumentative	arguably argumentatively
communicate	communication	communicative	
converse	conversation conversationalist	conversant	
defend	defense defender	defensive	defensively
deliberate	deliberation	deliberate	deliberately
enthuse	enthusiasm enthusiast	enthusiastic	enthusiastically
preserve	preserve preservation	preservative	
produce	product production producer	productive	productively
suppress	suppression suppressor	suppressive	
symbolize	symbol symbolism	symbolic	symbolically

Correct the sentences that have errors in word forms.

1. There are many <u>argumentatives</u> against drinking and driving.

2. I'm sure you misunderstood what he said. He wouldn't <u>deliberately</u> say something so insulting to you.

3. Martha is very <u>enthusiastically</u> about her new project.

4. Honest <u>communicative</u> is very important in all relationships.

5. Mehmet is a very good <u>conversation</u>. He always has interesting things to say.

6. The color red is often a <u>symbolic</u> of danger.

7. I believe we should try to <u>preservation</u> our valuable natural resources.

8. This was one of the most <u>produce</u> meetings we've had in a long time.

9. It is not always healthy to <u>suppress</u> your feelings of anger.

10. My husband usually acts <u>defensive</u> whenever I bring up the subject of money.

POSTREADING

DISCUSSION
QUESTIONS

1. What are some of the similarities and differences between your native language and English? For example, are the sentence structure and word order similar or different? What about the writing style? Is your language more or less formal than English?

2. North American author Richard Lederer said, "Not only are English's grammar and syntax relatively simple, the language's sound system is flexible and 'user friendly'—foreign words tend to be pronounced the same as in their original tongues. We have the most cheerfully democratic and hospitable language that ever existed. Other people recognize their language in ours."[4]

   Do you agree or disagree with Lederer's opinion? Respond to each of his points.

3. Linguist Anthony Burgess has said, "We have lost interest in language as an imaginative medium, and now we just write to communicate on the most basic possible level. People don't like literature. . . . The new view of language is the kid's view. It's just something you throw around. Slang is our substitute for poetry."[5] Do you agree with Burgess's opinion? Is what he says true in your country? Do you think this sounds like a problem between generations? What is your opinion about slang?

4. Do you think humans are the only animal capable of a sophisticated system of communication? Discuss the ways other animals communicate with each other.

5. Former Indian prime minister, Jawaharlal Nehru once said, "A living language is a throbbing, vital thing, ever-changing, ever-growing and mirroring the people who speak and write it. It has its roots in the masses, though its superstructure may represent the culture of a few." Why do you think Nehru chose these adjectives to describe language? How do you think language mirrors the people who speak and write it?

JUST FOR FUN

The following article tells about the history of punctuation. The first several lines are written the way they might have been in the past. Try to figure out what they mean and then read the whole history. Check your answer on page 229 of the Answer Key.

A·short·history·of PVNCTVATION BY

POLLY M. ROBERTVS

EARLYGREEKSHADHARDLYANYPUNCTUATION

FONOITCERIDEHTDEGNAHCNEVEDNA

THEIRWRITINGATTHEENDOFEACHLINELATER

TAHTGNITIRWFOYAWAOTDEGNAHCYEHT

FAVOREDRIGHTHANDEDPEOPLEANDSHOWED

WHEREANEWPARAGRAPHBEGANBYUNDERLINING

THEFIRSTLINEOFIT<u>LATERTHEGREEK</u>PLAYWRIGHT*

ARISTOPHANES•INVENTEDMARKSTOSHOW•WHERE

THEREADERSHOULDTAKEABREATH:

THE•ROMANS•MADE•WRITING•MUCH•EASIER•

TO•READ•BY•PUTTING•DOTS•BETWEEN•WORDS•

AND•BY•MOVING•THE•FIRST•LETTER•OF•A•

PARAGRAPH•INTO•THE•LEFT•MARGIN: THEY•

ADAPTED•SOME•OF•THE•GREEK•MARKS•SUCH•AS•

THE•COLON•MARK•TO•INDICATE•PHRASE•ENDINGS:

INTHEEARLYMIDDLEAGESTHISSYSTEMOFPUNCTUATION

BROKEDOWNBECAUSEVERYFEWPEOPLECOULDREAD

ANDWRITE   BUTWRITERSKEPTASPACEATTHEENDOF

ASENTENCEANDCONTINUEDTOMARKPARAGRAPHS

EVENTUALLY   WORDS   WERE   SEPARATED   AGAIN   AND

NEW SENTENCES BEGAN WITH A LARGER LETTER

* **playwright**   someone who writes plays.

The educational reforms of Charlemagne led to the invention of lowercase letters which could be written and read much faster/ Phrases and sentence endings were indicated either by ∴ or by a slash /

As time went on writers looked for more ways to clarify meaning / In medieval music notation they found a way to indicate how a voice should rise or fall at the end of a sentence or phrase ↗ Can you hear your voice rise at the end of a question? Our question mark came directly from medieval music notation ↗ When a long sentence broke in the middle > they put a new mark that became our semicolon and colon ↗ The hy= phen appeared as two lines instead of one ↗

Around A.D. 1500 the indented paragraph appeared, as did the comma and period as we know them. Printers of the Renaissance invented new marks like the exclamation point and quotation marks. By that time, people were commonly reading silently, and punctuation came to depend more on grammatical groups than breath groups. (Parentheses and dashes appeared with the advent of printing—these made text read more naturally to the inner ear.)

By the end of the seventeenth century, our punctuation system was in place for the most part, though sometimes details varied. Just think, though: After only a few lessons in school—and with lots of practice reading and writing—you can boast that you've mastered a system that took Westerners many centuries to develop!

READER'S JOURNAL

After you finish each unit in this book, you will have the opportunity to write for ten to twenty minutes in the space provided. This is called a reader's journal. You should feel free to use it to respond and react to the readings and activities in a personal way. You might want to consider writing about one of the quotes in this unit or answering one of the discussion questions. These journal entries are meant to help you reflect on and synthesize the information you have just read.

Now, begin writing on a topic of interest to you.

READER'S JOURNAL

Date: _____

_____

_____

_____

_____

_____

_____

_____

_____

_____

_____

_____

_____

_____

_____

_____

_____

_____

_____

_____

_____

_____

_____

_____

WINNING ISN'T EVERYTHING

Selections

Most of us would rather win than lose, and certainly success is sweeter than failure. The reality is, however, that we all lose sometimes. Learning how to put both winning and losing into perspective is something that comes with experience. Olympic marathon champion, Joan Benoit Samuelson captured this point when she said, "Winning is neither everything nor the only thing. It is one of many things."

1. Read the following statements and put a check mark next to those that apply to you. Discuss the results with your classmates.

_____ I am easily frustrated and tend to give up quickly.

_____ I am very determined and don't like to give up.

_____ Winning is very important to me.

_____ I hate to lose at anything.

_____ I am more concerned with fairness than winning or losing.

_____ I don't let obstacles get in my way.

_____ I meet every challenge with the attitude that I can win.

_____ I am obsessed with success.

_____ I don't care whether I win or lose, I just like to play the game.

_____ I come up with a lot of excuses when I don't win or succeed.

Florence Griffith-Joyner winning the 100-meter race in the 1988 Olympics in Seoul.

2. Sel Lederman, a psychiatrist who specializes in issues concerning losing has said, "Any experience in life, winning or losing, is only of significance if we learn from it. Usually, we learn more from losing than from winning." Do you agree that there is more to be learned from losing than from winning? What are some life lessons that losing can teach?

Pat Riley has been involved in team sports all his life. He played professional basketball for many years and has coached several pro teams including the Los Angeles Lakers, the New York Knicks, and the Miami Heat. In **What Winners Know,** Riley discusses his prescription for success in life. As many authors do, Riley begin's his article with a short personal story to catch the reader's attention: specifically, Riley sets the scene for the advice he wants to give by comparing a river-rafting trip he took to the trip of life.

BEFORE YOU READ

PREREADING QUESTIONS

1. What does it mean to be a winner in your culture? What are the outward signs of success?

2. In your culture, is it common for celebrities to write inspirational, self-help books? Have you ever read any?

3. Is the concept of being a team player important in your culture? In what areas is it important?

What Winners Know

BY   PAT   RILEY

1   One summer my wife Chris and I were invited by friends to paddle down the Colorado River in an inflatable raft. Our expedition included many highly successful people—the kind who have staffs to take care of life's menial chores. But in the wilder rapids, all of us instinctively set aside any pretenses and put our backs into every stroke to keep the raft from tumbling over. At each night's encampment, we all hauled supplies and cleaned dishes.

2   After only two days, the river became a great equalizer. People accustomed to being pampered and indulged had become a team, working together to cope with the unpredictable twists and turns of the river.

3   I believe that in life—as well as on raft trips—several truths will make all our journeys successful ones.

4   *Be a team player.* The rhythms of teamwork have been the rhythms of my life. I played basketball alongside Hall-of-Famers, and the team I now coach, the New York Knicks, has rebounded from years of adversity to become a major contender in the 1990s.

5   I'm persuaded that teamwork is the key to making dreams come true. We

Pat Riley coaching the New York Knicks.

all play on a number of teams in our lives—as part of a family, as a citizen, as a member of a congregation or a corporation. Every team has a covenant, written or unwritten. It contains the values and goals for every team member.

6   For example, in the late 1970s a General Motors plant in Fremont, Calif., was the scene of constant warfare between labor and management. Distrust ran so high that the labor contract was hundreds of pages of legal doublespeak. GM spent millions trying to keep the facility up to date, but productivity and quality were continually poor. Absenteeism was so out of control that the production line couldn't even start up on some mornings. Finally in the early 1980s, GM shut down the plant.

7   GM became convinced that it had to create new production systems based on teamwork. In the mid-1980s it reopened the Fremont plant in a joint venture with Toyota, starting from scratch with a much simpler and shorter labor contract. It promised that executive salaries would be reduced and jobs performed by outside vendors would be given to employees before any layoffs were considered. Over a hundred job classifications were cut to just two. Instead of doing one monotonous job over and over, workers agreed to be part of small teams, spending equal time on various tasks.

8   Absenteeism dropped about 85 percent. Today the plant generates close to 4300 jobs and pumps $800 million a year into the local economy. The great paradox is that by sacrificing superficial self-interests for the sake of your team, you can reap bigger rewards all around.

9   *Welcome change.* A friend of mine learned this lesson well. At 45, Lew Richfield felt he owed something to his community, so he volunteered at a suicide-prevention center in his spare time. Professional counselors there told him he had a talent for working with people and encouraged him to develop it.

10   Although he had a successful career as assistant to the chairman of a $140-million company, Lew's one regret was that he'd never gone to college. So at 46, he sold his house, and both he and his wife, Gloria, entered college; after graduating, they went on to earn their Ph.D.s and become full-time family therapists. Lew is the author of two books on aging and relationships—and a very happy man.

11   I truly believe that life is a series of constant changes, and while it may not be apparent at the time, they can help you learn and grow. For as Oliver Wendell Holmes, Sr., put it: "Every now and then a man's mind is stretched by a new idea or sensation, and never shrinks back to its former dimensions."

12   *Beware of complacency.* There is a temptation to slack off when you feel good about what you've achieved—to let go of yesterday's hunger and insecurity and to accept the illusion that your struggle has ended.

13   Professional athletes know the danger of complacency both in their professional and personal lives. Some reach their middle years and, when the adulation stops, settle into marginal careers. Some even hit bottom.

14 Those who survive are the ones who prepare for their post-glory days—like Dave Bing, who played for the Detroit Pistons in the mid-1960s. He was the league's leading scorer by his second year and is now considered one of basketball's all-time greats.

15 Thinking ahead was part of Bing's makeup. Before he played pro ball, he went to Syracuse University. Since he came from a poor background, his advisers figured him for a classroom dud and suggested he skip serious courses. Bing didn't buy into their thinking. He even continued his education during his pro years, reading voraciously on road trips, hustling off-season jobs at a bank, at Chrysler and at a steel company, and educating himself in the skills of business. Today, one of the most successful black businessmen in the country, Bing is CEO of three multimillion-dollar companies and has over 300 people on his payroll.

16 Any time you stop striving to get better, you're bound to get worse. As my friend Lew points out, "If you go to a baseball game and sit in the stands hoping a ball is going to get hit to you, you'll have to wait a very long time. You've got to get out on the field."

17 *Remember, attitude is the mother of luck.* Every life has its setbacks. Facing those setbacks is what keeps you alive.

18 That's a lesson Jan Scruggs began learning in May 1969 in South Vietnam when his infantry unit was attacked by the North Vietnamese. Scruggs had shrapnel wounds so serious he was sent home to recuperate. During his brief time in Vietnam, over half of the men in his company were killed or wounded.

19 After leaving the Army and entering college to get a degree in counseling, Scruggs dreamed of building a memorial to his fellow soldiers—but he let the idea drop. All he could think of were his limitations: he had no organization and no money.

20 Then in 1979 he saw *The Deer Hunter,* a powerful movie about the impact of Vietnam on a group of small-town friends. Scruggs couldn't sleep after seeing it. Memories of dead comrades came flooding back.

21 Now he was determined. He used his own money to register the Vietnam Veterans Memorial Fund as a nonprofit organization, and on May 28, 1979, ten years after he was injured, he held a press conference to announce his plans. Soon after he had assembled a tremendous volunteer force of fund-raisers.

22 In July 1980, the government set aside a site next to the Lincoln Memorial and gave Scruggs and his volunteers five years to raise money for construction. Veterans and families of those who died wrote Scruggs hundreds of letters of support and sent what money they could spare, mostly modest amounts of $20 or less. Three years ahead of schedule, on November 13, 1982, Scruggs attended the dedication services for the Vietnam Veterans Memorial.

23 I'm convinced that all great breakthroughs in life happen because they deny the crippling fear of failure. So listen to the inner voice that counsels courage, that affirms your life and your ability, and you will tap the power that makes a winner.

PAT RILEY was named the National Basketball Association's Coach of the Year for 1990 and 1993.

1. Riley mentions four truths involved in living successfully. In your own words, describe the four truths.

   a. *Be a team player:* _____

   _____

   b. *Welcome change:* _____

   _____

   c. *Beware of complacency:* _____

   _____

   d. *Remember, attitude is the mother of luck:* _____

   _____

2. Riley explains each of these truths by giving an anecdotal example. Refer back to the article and summarize each example in your own words.

   a. *Be a team player:* _____

   _____

   b. *Welcome change:* _____

   _____

   c. *Beware of complacency:* _____

   _____

   d. *Remember, attitude is the mother of luck:* _____

   _____

3. Reread the quote by Oliver Wendell Holmes, Sr., in paragraph 11. Discuss what new ideas have stretched your mind. Then rewrite the quote in your own words.

   _____

   _____

   _____

   _____

   _____

**BUILDING
WRITING SKILLS**

APPLICATION OF
INFORMATION

If you were writing an article about how to be successful in life, what four truths would you suggest? Describe them briefly below. Discuss your ideas with the rest of the class.

1. _____

_____

2. _____

_____

3. _____

_____

4. _____

_____

FIGURE IT OUT

IDIOMS

Complete the following sentences with an idiom from the list. Use the context from the paragraphs cited to help you figure out the meanings.

up to date (¶6)	start from scratch (¶7)	buy into (¶15)
out of control (¶6)	put it (¶11)	bound to (¶16)
shut down (¶6)	slack off (¶12)	let it drop (¶19)

1. If you want to get good grades, you shouldn't _____slack off_____ at the end of the semester.

2. Her spending habits were so _____ that her parents took away her credit card.

3. I don't _____ the mayor's new program for land development.

4. As Stanley _____ , sometimes you have to spend money to make money.

5. This is such a controversial topic that I think we should _____ for a while.

6. David _____ his first business completely

_____ and built it into an international company.

(continued on the next page)

7. The company _____ its factory in Georgia and opened one in Florida.

8. I need a technical dictionary that is _____ .

9. If Linda stays on her diet, she is _____ lose weight.

EXPANDING VOCABULARY

Circle the letter of the word that is closest in meaning to the italicized word in each sentence.

1. The word *instinctively* in paragraph 1 is closest in meaning to _____ .
   a. cautiously
   b. naturally
   c. frequently
   d. boldly

2. The word *adversity* in paragraph 4 is closest in meaning to _____ .
   a. misfortune
   b. achievement
   c. security
   d. determination

3. The word *cut* in paragraph 7 is closest in meaning to _____ .
   a. increased
   b. reduced
   c. paid
   d. owed

4. The word *monotonous* in paragraph 7 is closest in meaning to _____ .
   a. dangerous
   b. difficult
   c. exciting
   d. dull

5. The word *generates* in paragraph 8 is closest in meaning to _____ .
   a. sells
   b. accepts
   c. displays
   d. creates

6. The word *apparent* in paragraph 11 is closest in meaning to _____ .

    a. pleasant
    b. clear
    c. successful
    d. helpful

7. The word *stretched* in paragraph 11 is closest in meaning to _____ .

    a. confused
    b. poisoned
    c. expanded
    d. noted

8. The word *dimensions* in paragraph 11 is closest in meaning to _____ .

    a. size
    b. ability
    c. change
    d. career

9. The word *complacency* in paragraph 12 is closest in meaning to _____ .

    a. contentment
    b. resentment
    c. imitation
    d. illusion

10. The word *striving* in paragraph 16 is closest in meaning to _____ .

    a. standing
    b. aiding
    c. trying
    d. dreaming

11. The word *modest* in paragraph 22 is closest in meaning to _____ .

    a. important
    b. decent
    c. small
    d. proper

Hundreds of books have been written on the subject of winning, very few on losing.

No one likes to fail, but it is almost impossible to be a winner all the time. In **The Fine Art of Self-Handicapping,** you will read about some of the psychological tricks people use to protect themselves from the threat of failure.

1. Do you have any psychological tricks for avoiding failure? If so, what are they?

2. Do you make excuses for yourself when you do not succeed at something? Do you ever make excuses before you even try to do something? In what types of situations do you make excuses?

The Fine Art of Self-Handicapping

PSYCHOLOGICAL TRICKS FOR AVOIDING FAILURE

BY JOANNIE M. SCHROF

1   Bad luck always seems to strike at the worst possible moment. A man about to interview for his dream job gets stuck in traffic. A law student taking her final exam wakes up with a blinding headache. A runner twists his ankle minutes before a big race. Perfect examples of cruel fate.

2   Or are they? Psychologists who study such common mishaps now believe that in many instances, they may be carefully orchestrated schemes of the subconscious mind. In their new book, "Your Own Worst Enemy" (Basic Books, $21), Steven Berglas of Harvard Medical School and McLean Hospital in Belmont, Mass., and Roy Baumeister of Case Western Reserve University contend that people often engage in a form of self-defeating behavior known as self-handicapping—or, in plain terms, excuse making. It's a simple process: By taking on a crippling handicap, a person makes it more likely that he or she will fail at an endeavor. Though it seems like a crazy thing to do, Berglas and Baumeister say it is actually a clever trick of the mind, one that sets up

a win-win situation by allowing a person to save face when he or she does fail.

3   A classic self-handicapper is the French chess champion Deschapelles, who lived during the 18th century. Deschapelles was a phenomenal player who quickly became champion of his region. But when competition grew tougher, he adopted a new condition for all matches: He would compete only if his opponent would remove one of Deschapelle's pawns and make the first move, increasing the odds that Deschapelles would lose. If he did lose, he could blame it on the other player's advantage and no one would know the true limits of his ability; but if he won against such odds, he would be all the more revered for his amazing talents. Psychologists now use the term "Deschapelles coup" to refer to acts of self-sabotage rampant in today's world.

Excusing Men

4   Overall, men are more likely than women to make excuses. Several studies suggest that men feel the need to appear competent in all realms, while women worry only about the skills in which they've invested heavily. Ask a man and a woman to go scuba diving for the first time, and the woman is likely to jump in, while the man is likely to first make it known that he's not feeling too well.

5   Ironically, it is often success that leads people to flirt with failure. Praise garnered for mastering a skill—becoming the best trial lawyer in the state, wooing the most clients—suddenly puts one in the position of having everything to lose. Rather than putting their reputation on the line again, many successful people develop a handicap—drinking, fatigue, depression—that allows them to keep their status no matter what the future brings. One of Berglas's patients, an advertising executive hospitalized for depression shortly after winning an award, put it this way: "Without my depression, I'd be a failure now; with it, I'm a success 'on hold.'"

6   In fact, the people most likely to become chronic excuse makers are those obsessed with success, says Berglas, who is a consultant to several leading business executives. Such people are so afraid of being labeled a failure at anything that they constantly develop one handicap or another in order to explain away failure.

7   Though self-handicapping can be an effective way of coping with performance anxiety now and then, in the end, researchers say, it is a Faustian bargain*. Over the long run, excuse makers fail to live up to their true potential, thwart their own goals and lose the status they care so much about. And despite their protests to the contrary, they have only themselves to blame.

---

*   **Faustian bargain** An agreement that will bring the bargainer to ruin. Johann Faust was a sixteenth-century German doctor who performed magic and died mysteriously. According to legend he sold his soul to the devil in exchange for youth, knowledge, and magical power.

HOW WELL DID YOU READ

Circle the letter of the choice that best completes the sentence or answers the question.

1. Which of the following is the main topic of the article?

   a. a comparison between the ways men and women avoid failure
   b. the psychological tricks some people use to avoid failure
   c. the life of a classic self-handicapper, Deschapelles
   d. how trial lawyers and advertising executives avoid failure

2. The author feels that _____ .

   a. people obsessed with success are most likely to become chronic excuse makers
   b. self-handicapping is usually an effective method of coping with performance anxiety
   c. women are more likely to be self-handicappers than men
   d. people who often fail at their endeavors should practice self-handicapping

3. According to the passage, which of the following is not an example of self-handicapping?

   a. removing one of your pawns before a chess game
   b. twisting your ankle before an important race
   c. leaving in plenty of time for an important meeting
   d. getting stuck in traffic on the way to a job interview

4. It can be inferred from the passage that a student who wanted to engage in self-handicapping would _____ .

    a. study as hard as possible for a big exam
    b. try to cheat on a test to get a high score
    c. get drunk the night before a big test
    d. do extra-credit work for a course

5. The words *such people* in paragraph 6 refer to _____ .

    a. business executives
    b. chronic excuse makers
    c. people obsessed with success
    d. consultants

6. The word *it* in the last line of paragraph 5 refers to _____ .

    a. success
    b. failure
    c. handicap
    d. depression

7. Where does the author mention a book about self-handicapping?

    a. paragraph 1
    b. paragraph 2
    c. paragraph 3
    d. paragraph 5

8. Which of the following conclusions does the article support?

    a. Self-handicapping is ultimately a destructive behavior.
    b. Chronic excuse making is a sign of depression.
    c. Self-handicapping is an effective way to improve status.
    d. Self-handicapping is a difficult and complicated process.

9. The word *strike* in paragraph 1 is closest in meaning to which of the following?

    a. disappear
    b. adapt
    c. occur
    d. stop

10. The word *endeavor* in paragraph 2 is closest in meaning to which of the following?

    a. interview
    b. attempt
    c. event
    d. offer

BUILDING READING SKILLS
UNDERSTANDING POINT OF VIEW

Which of the following statements do you think the author would agree with? Put a check mark next to those statements.

_____ 1. Cruel fate is the only explanation for the bad luck that often strikes at the worst possible moment.

_____ 2. Self-handicapping is a way to protect oneself from failure.

_____ 3. Since women do not feel the need to be competent in all areas, they tend to make fewer excuses than men.

_____ 4. Many successful people develop a handicap such as drinking or depression to avoid having to put their reputation on the line.

_____ 5. Chronic excuse makers are often those people who are obsessed with failure.

_____ 6. All in all, self-handicapping is the best way of coping with performance anxiety.

EXPANDING VOCABULARY
DEFINING TERMS

Choose five words from this article that are new to you and teach them to your classmates. Present a definition and a sentence that uses the word in context for each one.

1. _____

_____

2. _____

_____

3. _____

_____

4. _____

_____

5. _____

_____

When you *paraphrase,* you rewrite something you have heard or read using your own words. Paraphrase the following sentences. Your sentence should express the main idea of the original sentence as clearly and simply as possible.

Example:

By taking on a crippling handicap, a person makes it more likely that he or she will fail at an endeavor.

When people use handicaps, they increase the chances of failure.

1. *Several studies suggest that men feel the need to appear competent in all realms, while women worry only about the skills in which they've invested heavily.*

_____

_____

_____

2. *Rather than putting their reputation on the line again, many successful people develop a handicap—drinking, fatigue, depression—that allows them to keep their new status no matter what the future brings.*

_____

_____

_____

3. *Over the long run, excuse makers fail to live up to their true potential, thwart their own goals, and lose the status they care so much about.*

_____

_____

_____

1. In your own words, explain the concept of self-handicapping.

2. Why do you think the author calls self-handicapping a "fine art"?

3. The article mentions several ways that people handicap themselves. Do you ever do any of these things?

4. The author states that success often leads people to flirt with failure. Do you think this is true? Have you ever flirted with failure? If so, when and why?

Most of us can point to someone in our lives who has served as a role model and source of strength and inspiration. In **What Makes a Champion,** Joe Lewis talks about his father and the life lessons he taught.

1. Look at the title of the article and discuss what you think makes a champion. What are the most important qualities of a winner?

2. At the beginning of the article, Joe Lewis asks, "What does it mean to grow old? What does it mean to age?" How would you answer these questions?

What Makes a Champion

I may not always be by you, but I'll always be with you.

By Joe Lewis

1   What does it mean to grow old? What does it mean to age?

2   Let me tell you about my father, John Gary Lewis. I remember him about the age of 50. Even then, he could work harder than—and outdo—men half his age. The fact that he never smoked or went to movies or parties made it easier for him, true. But he believed in working regardless of whether he was sick or injured. If he were coming down with a cold, instead of going to a doctor, he would buy a bag of oranges and sit down and eat nearly the whole bag.

3   The fact is, he almost never got sick and he never seemed to get hurt. He didn't believe in doctors. He was old-fashioned in every way: home care when you were sick, farming, you name it. He did his plowing behind mules because he thought tractors would damage the roots of the plants. He was a college professor in North Carolina for 30 years, full-time, and when he wasn't doing that, he was out at his farm, working, sunup to sundown, never taking a vacation, day in and day out, year after year.

4   So my four brothers and I grew up in Raleigh in a tough family, guided by the principle that physical strength and endurance are key to survival. I still think of my father at 50 on his feet in the hot burning sun, outworking my brothers and me.

5   A long time afterward, when I turned 50, I got into the ring and sparred four or five rounds with some young kids, three-minute rounds, and I found it quite easy to run them out of gas.

6   I also happen to have a 62-year-old friend, Gene LaBell, a movie stuntman and two-time national judo champion, who can go out on the mat and wrestle nonstop for a full hour. I've seen folks 70 and over who can press their body weight. And I know members of the Santa Monica track club—guys 48, 49 and 50 years old—who can still run the 100 meters in 10 seconds flat.

7   The trouble with most of us is that we're conditioned to start surrendering inside once we get between 50 and 60. Our values and interests start to change, and it no longer matters so much who's king of the hill, especially since we know it's unlikely to be us.

8   But why flush your skills and talents down the drain just because you're a little older? There's something in each of us—call it spirit, an essence, energy, confidence, courage, heart, guts, back-

bone, intensity, spunk, inner motor or just a plain old refusal to give up, like my old man. If you let this part of you begin to go to sleep, it will begin working on taking the rest of you to your grave.

9   I have found that each of us has an inner rhythm or gift, and often a great deal of it never even gets touched.

10   We have to learn to live with fear, whether it's fear of death, fear of injury, fear of failure or plain old fear of being laughed at because we're competing with folks half our age. Common sense and a little reflection make it plain that none of this means a thing.

11   When you are old, you can still be a winner, because winning truly means being the best of what you are, doing the best you can do, regardless of what anybody else says.

12   You don't give up. Like my father, who died at 68 and never gave up, and who has been my life's example. He is no longer by me, but he is always with me.

13   Never give up. Never.

Joe Lewis makes the following points in this article. Discuss your reactions to his ideas.

1. *The trouble with most of us is that we're conditioned to start surrendering inside once we get between 50 and 60.*

2. *I have found that each of us has an inner rhythm or gift, and often a great deal of it never even gets touched.*

3. *We have to learn to live with fear, whether it's fear of death, fear of injury, fear of failure...*

**BUILDING
READING SKILLS**

LOOKING AT STYLE

Joe Lewis writes in a very casual, conversational style. Much of the language he used in the article is informal and idiomatic. When you read the article, you almost feel as though he is talking to you. Below are several examples of Joe Lewis's use of informal language.

Rewrite the sentences in your own words.

1. *He was old-fashioned in every way: home care when you were sick, farming, you name it.*

_____

_____

_____

When Kristi
Yamaguchi fell on
the ice in the
1992 Winter
Olympics,
everyone
thought she had
lost her chances
for the gold
medal in figure
skating. But
Kristi did not
lose her
determination.
She got right
back up, started
skating, and went
on to win the
gold medal.

2. *When I turned 50, I got into the ring and sparred four or five rounds with some young kids, . . . and I found it quite easy to run them out of gas.*

_____

_____

_____

3. *Our values and interests start to change, and it no longer matters so much who's king of the hill . . .*

_____

_____

_____

4. *But why flush your skills and talents down the drain just because you're a little older?*

_____

_____

_____

5. *There's something in each of us—call it spirit, an essence, energy, confidence, courage, heart, guts, backbone, intensity, spunk, inner motor, or just a plain old refusal to give up, like my old man.*

_____

_____

_____

TALK IT OVER

DISCUSSION
QUESTIONS

1. Joe Lewis says that his father has been his life's example. Do you have someone that you consider your life's example? If so, describe that person and explain why he or she is such an important role model for you.

2. Joe Lewis grew up in a family that was guided by the principle that physical strength and endurance are key to survival. Do you agree with this principle? Does your family have a guiding principle? If so, what is it?

3. The article both begins and ends with the quote "I may not always be by you, but I'll always be with you." What do you think this means? Does this quote have significance for you?

PROVERBS

Read and discuss the following sayings about winning and losing. Think of some more to add to the list.

1. Don't put all your eggs in one basket.

2. Don't count your chickens before they hatch.

3. A bird in the hand is worth two in the bush.

4. It's no use crying over spilled milk.

5. It isn't whether you win or lose; it's how you play the game.

6. Look ahead or you'll find yourself behind.

7. All's fair in love and war.

Edgar Guest (1881–1959) is a British-born author who is known for his poetry about friendship and family life. **It Couldn't Be Done** is one of his best-loved poems.

Discuss the meanings of the words and phrases below with your teacher and classmates before you read the poem.

chuckle	buckle in	trace of a grin	quiddit
tackle	scoff	prophesy	assail

It Couldn't Be Done

BY EDGAR A. GUEST

Somebody said that it couldn't be done,
    But he with a chuckle replied
That "maybe it couldn't," but he would be one
    Who wouldn't say so till he'd tried.
5 So he buckled right in with the trace of a grin
    On his face. If he worried he hid it.
He started to sing as he tackled the thing
    That couldn't be done, and he did it.

Somebody scoffed: "Oh, you'll never do that;
10   At least no one ever has done it";
But he took off his coat and he took off his hat,
    And the first thing we knew he'd begun it.
With a lift of his chin and a bit of a grin,
    Without any doubting or quiddit,
15 He started to sing as he tackled the thing
    That couldn't be done, and he did it.

There are thousands to tell you it cannot be done,
    There are thousands to prophesy failure;
There are thousands to point out to you, one by one,
20   The dangers that await to assail you.
But just buckle in with a bit of a grin,
    Just take off your coat and go to it;
Just start to sing as you tackle the thing
    That "cannot be done," and you'll do it.

TALK IT OVER

DISCUSSION
QUESTIONS

1. In lines 1 and 9, the author uses the word *somebody*. Who do you think *somebody* refers to? Throughout the poem, the author refers to *he*. Who do you think *he* is supposed to be?

2. What do you think the author means when he says, "It couldn't be done?" What kinds of things is he referring to?

3. In the third stanza, the author says, "There are thousands to point out to you, one by one, the dangers that wait to assail you." What dangers do you think he is talking about?

4. Throughout history, people with new ideas and those who want to try new things have faced resistance from others. Who can you think of that would fit in this category? What kind of resistance did they face?

5. In your own words, tell the class what this poem means to you.

**BUILDING
READING SKILLS**

DISCOVERING
POETIC RHYTHM

The rhythm of "It Couldn't Be Done" is very regular and strong. Practice reading it out loud following the model of your teacher. Then practice reading sections of it with a partner.

**ACROSS TIME
AND CULTURES**

Read the following selection as quickly as possible and decide which title is the most appropriate. Write the title on the line.

1. Winner Takes All

2. Born to Lose

3. Dealing with Defeat

4. How to Change the World

There are many more ways to lose than there are to win. Losing is so much more interesting than winning. Winning isn't always worth its weight in blue ribbons, and losing can be positive and ennobling if it compels us to examine why we lost.

Have we forgotten that losers changed the world? Columbus missed his target by thousands of miles; Thomas Edison had most of his inventing triumphs before the age of 40 and, in his later years, rolled up an ever-increasing number of failures. Failure and poverty dogged Charles Goodyear all his life. Mozart died impoverished and was buried in the pauper's section of the church cemetery. Van Gogh was a suicide. Most of the first edition of *Walden* was remaindered into Thoreau's personal library. Churchill distracted himself from defeat with painting, writing, gardening, and breeding butterflies.[1]

WORD FORMS   Study the following chart of words that appeared in this unit.

VERB	NOUN	ADJECTIVE	ADVERB
	adversity adversary	adverse adversarial	adversely
determine	determination	determined	indeterminably
endure	endurance	endurable enduring	
execute	execution executor executive	executive	
indulge	indulgence	indulgent	indulgently
	instinct	instinctive	instinctively
	irony	ironic	ironically
obsess	obsession	obsessive obsessed	obsessively
oppose	opposition opposite	opposing	
predict	prediction predictor	predictable	predictably

Correct the sentences that have errors in word forms.

1. The <u>ironic</u> of the situation escaped him.

2. The committee <u>oppositions</u> the construction of a new stadium.

3. The president is the head of the <u>executive</u> branch of the government.

4. The Rosens are such <u>indulgence</u> parents that their children are very spoiled.

5. A true friend will stand by you even in times of <u>adversity</u>.

6. He worked <u>obsessive</u> on his paper until every detail was perfect.

7. I didn't like the movie because every scene was so <u>predictably</u>.

8. We are born with a natural <u>instinctive</u> for survival.

9. A basic rule of economics is that demand <u>determines</u> supply.

10. I can't <u>endurance</u> listening to that barking dog another minute.

Read and discuss the following opinions about the meaning of winning and losing, success and failure.

1. "The purpose of life is to be defeated by greater and greater things." (Rainer Maria Rilke)

2. You're not finished when you lose. You're only finished when you quit.

3. "Be nice to people on your way up because you'll meet them on the way down." (Wilson Mizner)

4. "Success has ruined many people." (Ben Franklin)

5. "Try not to become a man of success, but rather try to become a man of value." (Albert Einstein)

6. Many people have turned their worst failures into their biggest successes.

Look at the word *self-handicapping*. **It contains sixteen letters. Using only these sixteen letters, make as many other words as you can. You may not use the same letter twice unless it appears twice in the word** *self-handicapping*. **Do not use proper names or foreign words.**

_____	_____	_____
_____	_____	_____
_____	_____	_____
_____	_____	_____
_____	_____	_____
_____	_____	_____
_____	_____	_____

Choose a topic that relates to the readings in this unit and write for about ten to twenty minutes. Consider writing about one of the quotes in this unit or answering one of the discussion questions.

READER'S JOURNAL

Date: _____

WHAT IS ART?

FYi

Unit·3

Selections

If you ask ten people, "What is art?" you will probably get ten different answers. Art means different things to different people. To some people, art is the product of creativity. To others, art represents something religious or even political. To still others, art is about high culture, status, and even financial investments.

Think about and then discuss the following questions.

1. While you read the following paragraph about art, consider what art means to you.

> Society has encouraged art since the beginning of time; it is a treasure that we inherit from the past, add to in the present, and then give to the future. But what exactly is art? Why is it so difficult to define? Art is something that appeals to our senses. No one can tell us what to like or dislike about a piece of art. Art is something different to each of us because we each bring our own backgrounds, experiences, beliefs, and expectations to art. We respond to a work of art emotionally, but we also respond intellectually; we each have our own standards of beauty and satisfaction.

What do you think a good definition of art might be? Think about it for a few minutes and then write a definition.

To me, art means _____

_____

2. Do you have any hobbies that involve the visual arts? For example, do you like to paint, draw, or take pictures? What types of art do you enjoy most?

3. What types of art or crafts are traditional in your culture? Describe them to your classmates or bring in some pictures to show.

The importance of the arts is often minimized in education. The following essay, **The Arts *Are* Essential,** was written by an art teacher to help parents and educators understand the important role that the arts play in the education of children.

BEFORE YOU READ

PREREADING QUESTIONS

1. Is art instruction emphasized in your country? How much time is devoted to it each week? How much time do you think should be devoted?

2. How important do you think art instruction is? In what ways can instruction in the arts benefit children? What life skills can be learned from studying art?

BUILDING READING SKILLS

PREVIEWING

There are several steps you can take to improve your reading comprehension skills. One of the most important of these, **previewing,** is something you should do *before* you actually read the article. When you preview a text, you examine certain parts of it before you read it all the way through. You can gather clues about the article from the title, subtitle, pictures, charts, and headings.

The process of previewing gives you a general idea of the content of the text. When you have some idea about the content before you read, you have a better understanding of what you are reading. Previewing will also give you clues about how the text is organized. It will help you anticipate the sequence of information. Finally, previewing should give you a sense of the level of difficulty of the text.

> Previewing will give you a good idea of what you are about to read and how you should approach reading it.

Here are some steps to follow when you preview an article. Use them as a guideline for previewing "The Arts *Are* Essential."

1. Look at the title of this article and write it on the lines below. The title usually gives you a good idea of what the article is about. Think about what it means and try to make some predictions about the content of the article.

   _____

   _____

2. Read the subtitle. A subtitle is right under the title and is important because it often summarizes the main point of the article. Write the subtitle below and think about what the main point of the article might be.

   _____

   _____

(continued on the next page)

3. Read the first and last paragraphs of the article. The first paragraph may serve as an introduction to the subject and help you understand the purpose of the article. The last paragraph often contains conclusions or summarizes the information. Together these two paragraphs can provide a general overview of the whole article.

4. Examine the headings that appear throughout the text and write them below. They will give you hints about the main points that the author presents. The headings will help you guess the content of each section. They may also show you how the article is organized.

_____

_____

_____

_____

_____

_____

After you read each heading, try to predict the content of each section. Then figure out how the sections relate to each other.

5. Look at any pictures, photographs, diagrams, and charts that appear throughout the article. Visual aids often highlight important concepts. This article contains one picture. Look at it, read the caption, and try to predict why the author included it.

6. Read the first sentence of each paragraph. This is frequently the topic sentence and gives the main idea of the paragraph.

7. Finally, read the whole article one time quickly. Do not stop to look up words in a dictionary, and do not spend time rereading parts you do not understand. The purpose of this first reading is just to get a general sense of the article and prepare you for a more careful reading.

8. Now that you have previewed the article, you should have a pretty good idea of its contents. Write a short prediction of what you think the article will be about.

_____

_____

Now, read the whole article carefully, and do the exercises that follow.

The Arts *Are* Essential

INSTRUCTION IN THE ARTS BUILDS SKILLS THAT TODAY'S STUDENTS MUST HAVE TO SUCCEED.

BY DEBRA COOPER-SOLOMON

1   The arts in education have often been considered a frill, something to entertain us, but not important enough to achieve the status of the academic areas of math, science and reading. There are many individuals who are skeptical about the practical benefits of arts study. These are the kinds of attitudes art educators must counter if art education is to take a more central role in the school curriculum. As an art teacher, I have long been aware of the important role the arts play in a child's development. I strongly believe the arts are an essential and fundamental part of a child's education.

Vital Tool in Building Self-Esteem

2   During the past eight years teaching the visual arts in both public and private school settings, I have seen how the arts can be a vital tool in building self-esteem and how they can be used to stimulate and facilitate academic learning. This is a topic of critical importance in an age of budgetary constraints, where many schools are facing a reduction or total elimination of arts programs. Research by cognitive psychologists and the experience of schools that include the arts as a part of the basic curriculum, strongly suggest that this reduction will not produce the results intended.

3   According to Eric Oddleifson, President of the Center for the Arts in the Basic Curriculum, arts education does a lot more that just enhance the traditional curriculum.

4   "The arts should be the basis of education, because the deepest and most lasting learning is participatory and whole-brained. This is precisely what the arts offer," Oddleifson said.

Cultivating Creativity, Discipline and Teamwork

5   Research into the records of several schools indicates that a curriculum that devotes 25 percent or more of the school day to the arts produces youngsters with academically superior abilities. Many advocates now argue that instruction in the arts cultivates creativity, discipline, and teamwork, skills that today's students must have to succeed both during and after completing school.

6   "Many people do not associate the arts with 'thinking.' We are aware of the art 'product'—the song, the picture, the play—but less aware of

ELKINS PARK SCHOOL

JUSTIN BERGER

HANDBOOK

An eleven-year-old student used his strength in visuo-spatial intelligence to design the cover for his school's handbook.

the 'process' which creates the product," said Oddleifson.

7   "The arts are not so much a result of inspiration and innate talent as they are a person's capacities for creative thinking and imagining, problem solving, creative judgment and a host of other mental processes. The arts represent forms of cognition every bit as potent as the verbal and logical/mathematical forms of cognition that have been the traditional focus of public education."

The Seven Intelligences

8   Psychologist Howard Gardner, places the arts firmly in the cognitive domain. Gardner believes we learn not just through the linguistic and mathematical methods of schooling, but through seven intelligences: logical/mathematical, verbal/linguistic, visual/spatial, body/kinesthetic, musical/rhythmic, intrapersonal and interpersonal. Because of the variety in learning styles, schools must teach students through all forms of intelligence. Through an understanding of Gardner's theory of multiple intelligences, we are now starting to appreciate the diverse ways in which children learn.

9   Mara Krechevsky, an associate of Gardner's at Harvard, tells the story of a first grader who loved to take things apart and put them together, but who wouldn't write in his journal at school. His spatial-mechanical strength outstripped his linguistic ability until his teacher suggested that he create a "tool dictionary" in which every entry consisted of a drawing of a tool and the word for it. In time, the child wrote whole sentences about tools and eventually became a leader who began to help other kids. In this boy's case, tools and his spatial and kinesthetic intelligences were an entry or a bridge to an area of difficulty.

Working from a Child's Strengths

10   "If a child feels better about himself because he is experiencing success in one area, that may just spill over into other activities," Krechevsky said.

11   The teachers Krechevsky talked with who have worked with Multiple Intelligence Theory spoke of this "spillover" in terms of greater risk-taking

by students. Given a chance to learn through the various domains of intelligences, children tend to try what is harder for them, because they have experienced success in easier areas. Multiple Intelligence Theory helps a teacher work from a child's strengths.

12   My work during the past four years has been as a teacher of the visual arts at the Learning Prep School, a school for language-impaired and learning-disabled students. Gardner's theory puts into words what I have long suspected to be true—there are many different ways of learning, and the arts are an area where some students can excel.

Achieving Success through the Visual Arts

13   The children at the Learning Prep School in West Newton, Massachusetts, have not succeeded in the traditionally accepted areas of intelligence (logical/mathematical and verbal/linguistic). These students are, however, capable of conceptual thinking, even though their use of language is often limited. The visual arts have been one of the areas in which a number of students have been able to succeed. The visual arts have been integrated into the traditional curriculum in order to enhance learning and to build on a child's strengths.

14   In many ways, the arts can help shape the total child. The visual arts encourage and stimulate language development, and promote conversations that eventually lead to a greater willingness and ability to express oneself verbally. Vocabulary building can very naturally be brought into the discussion of art projects by using words that describe color, texture, shape and size. Auditory skills of listening and following directions are reinforced. In addition, many children increase their power of observation and become more aware of the world around them. They can learn to concentrate and sustain interest in something meaningful to them. By using tools and materials, children increase manipulative skills, dexterity and coordination. They learn to make decisions of personal taste, color and materials, and they learn to share through creative expression.

Exercising Creativity

15   The arts also teach children that not all problems have a single correct answer. This is a different lesson from much of what is taught in the primary grades where many of the basic skills have only one correct answer to any question. The arts teach students the importance of using imagination, multiple perspective, and personal interpretation. Instead of demands of conformity, the arts enable children to think and exercise creativity.

16   The evidence is compelling that when the arts are treated as a serious academic subject, as well as when they are integrated into the standard academic curriculum, we create the right environment in which a child can learn, and we are better preparing our children for the present and future world.

Circle the letter of the choice that best completes the sentence or answers the question.

1. The article mainly discusses _____ .

    a. how to teach an art class
    b. the importance of art in education
    c. the theory of multiple intelligences
    d. budgetary constraints in the public schools

2. According to the article, many schools are reducing or eliminating their art programs because _____ .

    a. there are few qualified art teachers
    b. not enough students are interested in taking art courses
    c. art is not a valuable skill for students to learn
    d. they are experiencing budgetary constraints

3. The author included the example of a first grader who created a "tool dictionary" to _____ .

    a. demonstrate how spatial and kinesthetic intelligences can be used as a bridge to an area of difficulty
    b. prove that some children are greater risk-takers than others
    c. show that art can shape the total child
    d. prove that children can increase manipulative dexterity and coordination by using tools

4. According to the author, one thing that children can learn from studying art is _____ .

    a. there is a right and wrong way of doing everything
    b. the theory of multiple intelligences
    c. not all problems have a single correct answer
    d. imagination is not as important as intelligence

5. Which of the following is not an example of one of the seven intelligences?

    a. visual/spatial
    b. musical/rhythmic
    c. verbal/linguistic
    d. artistic/creative

6. Research from several studies shows that a curriculum that devotes at least one-fourth of the day to the arts produces _____ .

    a. children with superior academic skills
    b. classes that are easier to manage
    c. individuals who are skeptical about the practical benefits of art
    d. students with lower linguistic ability

7. The word *they* in paragraph 7 refers to _____ .

    a. the arts
    b. a person's capacities
    c. mental processes
    d. academic skills

BUILDING READING SKILLS

UNDERSTANDING POINT OF VIEW

Which of the following statements do you think the author would agree with? Put a check mark next to those statements.

_____ 1. While art classes stimulate students' creativity, there are not many practical benefits of arts study.

_____ 2. The arts can be helpful in building self-esteem.

_____ 3. When schools are trying to save money, they should reduce the amount spent on arts programs.

_____ 4. Instruction in the arts teaches students the skills they need to succeed both in school and out of school.

_____ 5. Although there are a variety of learning styles, some are more important than others.

_____ 6. All problems have one correct answer.

_____ 7. The visual arts can promote language development.

BUILDING READING SKILLS

EXAMINING SUPPORT

The author strongly believes that the arts are an essential part of a child's education. She supports her opinion with many reasons. Go through the article and make a list of her reasons. Which reasons do you agree with? Which ones do you disagree with. Discuss your opinions with your classmates.

_____

_____

_____

_____

_____

_____

_____

_____

A. Using contextual clues, write an approximate definition or synonym for the highlighted words in the sentences below. Then explain how the context helped you arrive at your answer.

1. *The arts in education have often been considered a **frill,** something to entertain us, but not important enough to achieve the status of the academic areas...*

   _____

   _____

2. *There are many individuals who are **skeptical** about the practical benefits of arts study. These are the kinds of attitudes art educators must counter if art education is to take a more central role in the school curriculum.*

   _____

   _____

3. *Through an understanding of Gardner's theory of multiple intelligences, we are now starting to appreciate the **diverse** ways in which children learn.*

   _____

   _____

4. *Gardner's theory puts into words what I have long **suspected** to be true—there are many different ways of learning, and the arts are an area where some students can excel.*

   _____

   _____

5. ***Auditory** skills of listening and following directions are reinforced.*

   _____

   _____

Vincent Van Gogh sold only one of his paintings during his lifetime—for $80. In 1988, his *Irises* was sold at auction for $54 million.

6. *By using tools and materials, children increase manipulative skills, **dexterity** and coordination.*

_____

_____

7. *The arts teach students the importance of using imagination, multiple perspectives, and personal interpretation. Instead of demands of **conformity**, the arts enable children to think and exercise creativity.*

_____

_____

8. *The evidence is **compelling** that when the arts are treated as a serious academic subject, . . . we create the right environment in which a child can learn . . .*

_____

_____

B. The following sentences contain vocabulary words from the previous exercise. Put a check mark next to the sentences that use the vocabulary word correctly.

_____ 1. I don't want to spend very much money on a car, so I am going to buy a standard model without any *frills*.

_____ 2. Everyone was very confident that Lee would win the tennis match. They were *skeptical* about her abilities.

_____ 3. The wildlife in Australia is very *diverse*.

_____ 4. I have always *suspected* that Jorge would be an excellent teacher.

_____ 5. Frank is an *auditory* learner. He needs to be able to see something in order to understand it.

_____ 6. Jane plays the piano with great *dexterity*.

_____ 7. Some cultures require *conformity* to rules more than others.

_____ 8. In his speech, the Mayor presented a *compelling* argument for the need to raise city taxes.

**BUILDING
WRITING SKILLS**

SUMMARIZING

Write a few sentences that summarize the main idea of "The Arts *Are* Essential" on the lines below. Then check to see how close your summary is to your original prediction on page 54.

_____

_____

_____

_____

_____

_____

TALK IT OVER

DISCUSSION
QUESTIONS

1. In your own words, explain Howard Gardner's theory of multiple intelligences. Then discuss how it can be applied to an educational curriculum.

_____

_____

_____

_____

_____

2. According to the author, a heavier emphasis on the arts in a curriculum produces students with academically superior abilities. Why does she think this is true? Do you agree with her?

3. The art program is often one of the first to be cut when a school is having financial difficulties. Why do you think this happens? Do you agree or disagree with this tendency.

Pablo Picasso, the Spanish painter and sculptor, is generally considered the great-est artist of the twentieth century. Some of his paintings have sold for millions of dollars. The following article, **Art Buyers May Not Care If Picasso Was a Monster,** discusses the impact a book about his life could have on the value of his work.

BEFORE YOU READ

PREREADING QUESTIONS

1. Have you ever seen any of Picasso's work in a museum or a book? What is your impression of his work?

2. If you had enough money, would you be interested in investing in art? What kind of artwork would you buy? Do you think art is a good financial investment?

3. Do you think this cartoon is funny? Explain why or why not.

"This next painting is from the 19th-century 'American School' and is claimed by critics and historians to be an excellent investment with continuous growth and long-range yield."

Art Buyers May Not Care If Picasso Was A Monster

BY JUDY DOBRZYNSKI

1 For many people, figuring out the modern art market can be as complicated as interpreting the art itself. Things have become even more confusing—or clear-cut, depending on your point of view—with the publication of *Picasso: Creator and Destroyer.* The author, Arianna Stassinopoulos Huffington, portrays him as a manipulative monster—particularly in his later years. And she has sparked a spirited debate over the value of his work.

2 In prose sometimes more purple than any Picasso painting, Huffington details the artist's cruelties toward his wives, mistresses, children, and friends. He once put out a cigarette on the cheek of his mistress Françoise Gilot, and he beat another, Dora Maar. Huffington says the sadism crept into the art, and once people understand that, she implies, they'll devalue much of his late work. In fact, she says, two collectors have already sold some works after reading her book.

PICASSO, Pablo. *Guernica.* 1937.

3 **OLD NEWS.** Art experts are crying foul, attacking the author's bias and lack of scholarship. As Diane Upright, a director at New York's Jan Krugier Gallery, says: "There's power in the work. Whether this was a gentle, sympathetic human being is irrelevant." Robert Rosenblum, an authority on modern art at New York University, is just as dismissive. "Anyone so ignorant as to sell his Picassos because of this book doesn't deserve to have them in the first place," he says.

4 Yet even the art world is finding it hard to ignore the Picasso potboiler: One day, while a gallery expert was vigorously denouncing the book as "trash journalism," the receptionist was avidly reading it under his desk. Partly because it's so controversial, the book seems headed for the bestseller list.

5 Still, Huffington's opus is likely to have far more success enlivening conversations than depressing prices. Most of its contents have been known to Picasso experts for years—with no deleterious effect on prices. "In his late years, everyone knows that Picasso was inordinately frustrated about his age, death, his loss of sexuality—that's in all of his work," says financier Asher Edelman, who owns several Picassos. "People will not stop buying Picassos because he was not a nice man." Rosenblum points out many artists have been scoundrels—or worse. Caravaggio, for one, killed a man in duel.

6 If it has any effect at all, the book may help prices. "Bringing more attention to Picasso will increase the attention given to his art, and therefore to the market," say Edelman.

7 Picasso's early works—up until about 1930—generally fetch higher prices than his late work, which is much more uneven. It includes many items he dashed off—and they look it. For many years Picasso's work was also seen as out of step with "mainstream" postwar art, according to Rosenblum. More recently, though, the more autobiographical and personal style that Picasso favored has again become popular. "The market for his late work has picked up enormously in the past two years," says John Tancock of Sotheby's.

8 **LATER WORKS.** Many of Picasso's works aren't as expensive as you might think. At a May sale at Sotheby's prices ranged from $15,400 for a 1940 pencil drawing of horses to $4.4 million for a 1901 painting entitled *Bust of a Woman Smiling*.

9 Works by Picasso regularly come up for sale at Sotheby's and Christie's. Also, search the New York galleries. Through July, Jan Krugier is showing late works inherited by Picasso's granddaughter Marina. It includes graphics, such as a 1959 etching of a reclining nude for $3,500, and paintings ranging from $250,000 to $2.5 million.

10 Nearby Pace Gallery represents three other heirs (son Claude, daughter Paloma, and grandson Bernard). On view are a color aquatint titled *Fumier,* priced at $17,000 and a linoleum-cut print of two nude lovers, dated 1963, priced at $10,000. Saidenburg Gallery offers prints, etchings, and aquatints ranging from $2,000 to $10,000. Perls Gallery has earlier and pricier works.

Read the following statements. If a statement is true, write *T* on the line. If it is false, write *F*.

_____ 1. Understanding the modern art market is more complicated than interpreting the works of art.

_____ 2. In her book, *Picasso: Creator and Destroyer,* Arianna Huffington describes Picasso in a very positive way.

_____ 3. Art critics are not supportive of Ms. Huffington's views on Picasso.

_____ 4. Many people will probably read the book because it is controversial.

_____ 5. The author of the article feels that the book will cause the prices of Picasso's paintings to go down.

_____ 6. Picasso's early works usually sell for more than his later works.

Decide if the following pairs of words are synonyms or antonyms. If they are synonyms, circle *S*. If they are antonyms, circle *A*.

1. clear-cut	confusing	S	A
2. portrays	represents	S	A
3. bias	prejudice	S	A
4. scoundrel	villain	S	A
5. irrelevant	pertinent	S	A
6. deleterious	harmful	S	A

Many idioms have more than one meaning. The first sentence in each of the groups below is taken from the article. Using contextual clues, write a definition of the highlighted idiom as it is used in the sentence. Then circle the letter of the sentence that uses the idiom in the same way.

1. *He once **put out** a cigarette on the cheek of his mistress…*

_____

a. It took a long time for the fire fighters to *put out* the forest fire.
b. Mary was so *put out* with her sister's inconsiderate behavior that she didn't talk to her for a week.
c. Our university *puts out* a weekly newspaper.

2. *Partly because it's so controversial, the book seems* **headed for** *the bestseller list.*

On May 8, 1995, Picasso's *Angel Fernandez de Soto* was sold at auction for $29 million. The next day, a Picasso from his Blue Period sold for $5 million.

   a. We left late last night and *headed for* Florida.
   b. Our committee needs a new *head for* next year.
   c. Mrs. Griffin *heads* the finance committee *for* the organization.

3. *Picasso's early works … generally fetch higher prices than his late work, which is much more uneven. It includes many items he* **dashed off**—*and they look it.*

   a. I'm late for work; I've got to *dash off* now.
   b. This sentence is not correctly punctuated. It should have a *dash*.
   c. I need to write my parents a long letter, but since I don't have much time right now, I'll just *dash off* a short note.

4. *The market for his late work has* **picked up** *enormously in the past two years.*

   a. My roommate always *picks* me *up* after class and drives me to work.
   b. He's been studying hard and his grades have finally begun to *pick up*.
   c. I've never studied Spanish formally, but I *picked up* enough when I was in Venezuela to get around.

5. *Works by Picasso regularly* **come up** *for sale at Sotheby's and Christie's.*

   a. The topic of marriage didn't *come up* for discussion until we had been dating for three years.
   b. The question is very difficult, and I can't *come up* with a good answer.
   c. The water at this end of the pool is very shallow. It only *comes up* to my knees.

TALK IT OVER

DISCUSSION QUESTIONS

1. Do you think an artist's personal life is relevant in evaluating his or her work? What examples can you think of to illustrate your point of view.

2. People love gossip. How do you think gossip about a well-known person affects the sales of his or her product, whether it is a painting, book, movie, song, or anything else?

3. Do you think that people are generally more interested in artists' lives or their works?

Read the following selection as quickly as possible and decide which title is the most appropriate. Write the title on the line.

1. Cubism: A Revolutionary Style in Art   3. A Rebel and His Art

2. Painting in Paris   4. The Influence of Art

No artist has affected modern art more than Pablo Picasso. The thousands of masterpieces he created changed the way people thought about art. Picasso was perhaps the most talented and successful artist who ever lived.

Pablo Ruiz Picasso was born in 1881 in a small town on the southern coast of Spain. His father was a painter who taught art. Picasso showed exceptional talent at an early age and, by the time he was in his teens, painted better than his father or any of the local art teachers. At sixteen, Picasso was sent to the Royal Academy of Madrid, where students drew from plaster casts and copied works of the old masters. Picasso felt these assignments were pointless and began to work on his own. Picasso's father soon became angry with his son's rebellious behavior, long hair, and strange clothes. He believed that Picasso was wasting his talent and scolded him, "Why don't you cut your hair and paint sensibly?"

In 1900, Picasso left for Paris—then the center of the art world. He lived in a cold, run-down building, painting constantly, sometimes surviving for days on only a piece of bread. During these years, his art reflected his dismal surroundings. Homeless outcasts were the subject of many of his fairly realistic early paintings. After seeing African masks and sculptures, his works became more simplified and angular leading up to the revolutionary new style known as Cubism.

Picasso didn't sell much of his work during these early years. But he worked continuously, always experimenting with different styles of painting. Though Picasso lived to be ninety-two and became the most famous artist in the world, he spoke of his youthful days in Paris as "the happiest time in my life."

After narcotics smuggling, art theft is the second most frequently committed international crime. Stolen works of art are often very difficult to track down, especially when they are well known. Since legitimate art collectors and dealers usually refuse to buy them, many stolen works simply disappear into the thriving underground art market. Others are destroyed in a desperate attempt to get rid of the evidence. Still others are eventually found in unlikely places. In **They're Stealing Our Masterpieces,** you will read about some of the biggest art thefts in history.

BEFORE YOU READ

PREREADING
QUESTIONS

1. Art theft is big business. Are you familiar with the facts surrounding any major art thefts? Were the works ever recovered?

2. What punishment do you think is justified for art theft? Do you think it is a more serious crime to steal a work of art or a car? Defend your answer.

They're Stealing Our Masterpieces

These works of art may be in a drug lord's den or awaiting sale at a church bazaar.

By Ira Chinoy

1 Last March thieves posing as police officers talked their way into Boston's Isabella Stewart Gardner Museum and pulled off the biggest art theft in history. The early-morning heist netted 13 art treasures valued at $200 million or more. Among them were "The Concert," one of more than 30 paintings by the 17th-century Dutch master Jan Vermeer, and Rembrandt's "Storm on the Sea of Galilee," his only known seascape.

2 Considering how risky it is to sell or hold for ransom a major work of art, the number of important pieces stolen is astonishing. Interpol, the international organization of police, knows of at least 39 works of Rembrandt stolen

The Concert by Vermeer, stolen March 1990

since 1981. Even more astonishing—in fact, one of the great mysteries of the art world—is that many masterpieces, too hot to sell and too dangerous to show off, have never resurfaced.

3   Huntington Block, a leading art insurer, says the recovery rate for important works is perhaps 50 percent . That's better than the ten-percent recovery rate for lesser known works of art. But it still leaves a lot of masterpieces unaccounted for.

4   The more famous the work, the more dangerous it is to sell. The goal of most thieves is to steal something valuable enough to be worth their while but obscure enough to get back inconspicuously into the legitimate art market.

5   "If it were known how many legitimate collectors, dealers and museums have dealt unknowingly in stolen art, there would be a lot of shaking of heads," says Milton Esterow, editor and publisher of the magazine *ARTnews.*

6   In some cases, the thieves have held the art for ransom. In October 1989, two thieves who tried to ransom three van Goghs for $2.5 million were sentenced to prison for 3 1/2 and five years respectively; the paintings, worth up to $100 million, had been taken in the Netherlands' biggest art heist.

7   One of the most bizarre cases of art theft, detailed in *The Art Stealers,* a book by Esterow, began in 1961. A visitor to London's National Gallery hid when the museum closed for the night and made off, through a bathroom window, with Goya's painting "The Duke of Wellington." The portrait had created a stir just weeks earlier when the British

government deemed it a national treasure and paid what was then an astounding sum, $392,000, to keep a wealthy American from obtaining it.

8   In his ransom demand, the thief asked for money not for himself but for charity. Over the next 3 1/2 years, similar demands were made. All were unsuccessful.

9   Finally, nearly four years after the painting was stolen, it was left anonymously, without the frame, at a railway baggage office. A 61-year-old taxi driver later confessed. He was convicted of stealing the frame, but cleared of stealing the painting and got three months in jail.

10   While the Goya was missing there was no shortage of theories about who was responsible. It even got a passing reference in the 1962 James Bond movie *Dr. No* when the British secret agent spotted what appeared to be Goya's portrait of the Duke of Wellington on display in the evil Dr. No's Caribbean hideaway.

11   The "Dr. No" theory has been bandied about ever since, as one spectacular art heist after another leaves art experts and police scratching their heads over the fate of so much missing worldclass art. Many experts say there's little solid evidence that missing masterpieces are hanging on the walls of real-life criminals. But others disagree.

12   FBI agent James D. Keith, who has worked cases in Florida and Texas, believes that some masterpieces are in the hands of South American narcotics dealers. "Money is nothing to them," says Keith. "But they like to have things that nobody else has."

13   There are less exotic scenarios to explain why a lot of fine art just disappears. "Many times the thief doesn't realize that art, unlike jewelry and other

Storm on the Sea of Galilee by Rembrandt, stolen March 1990

commodities, cannot be easily fenced," says Los Angeles Police Detective William E. Martin, one of three police officers in the country investigating art theft full time. "He can't sell it, so he may throw it in his basement or destroy it because he doesn't want to get caught with the evidence."

14 There was just such a case in 1988 in Huntington, N.Y. Manet's "Bouquet de Pivoines," valued at between $1 million and $5 million, was stolen from the Heckscher Museum. Three days later, the thief called the police. He claimed he had taken the painting on impulse and now realized that he would never be able to sell it. He told police they could recover the painting in the laundry room of a New York City apartment building. The police searched but couldn't find the missing Manet.

15 Two workmen had already found the canvas wrapped in a quilt behind a dryer. Later the building superintendent thought about hanging the painting in his apartment, but decided to leave it in a storage room. The police eventually located the missing work and described the superintendent as "a little shocked" when he found out what he had.

16 Then there was the case of a $50,000 Colonial American painting that surfaced in 1984—on sale for $90 at a church antiques show in Lynn, Mass. The painting had been snatched two years earlier in Boston. The antiques dealer who put it up for sale reportedly told police her son had bought it for $25 from a man selling paintings from the trunk of his car.

17 Milton Esterow tells of a Raphael painting stolen from a chapel in Rome. Lost or discarded by the thief, it fell into the hands of an Italian peasant. Years later, it was discovered being used to cover a broken window.

18 Such incidents give hope that if important stolen works are not destroyed they will show up sooner or later—and often where you would least expect them.

19 Sadly, art theft is on the rise. New York's International Foundation for Art Research, which monitors stolen art, received 5,000 reports last year, compared with 3,000 to 4,000 a year in the early 1980s.

20 Anne Hawley, director of the Gardner Museum, believes that current punishment for art thefts is too mild. "We would like to see stiff penalties for stealing national treasures," she says, "These belong to civilization."

HOW WELL DID YOU READ?

Read the following statements. If a statement is true, write *T* on the line. If it is false, write *F*.

_____ 1. Many stolen masterpieces seem to disappear.

_____ 2. It is more dangerous to sell famous works of art than to sell unknown works.

_____ 3. The goal of most art thieves is to steal the most valuable work possible.

(continued on the next page)

_____ 4. Only a few legitimate art dealers have ever bought stolen art.

_____ 5. Because of the strict punishment for art theft, there are fewer cases of stolen art than ever before.

BUILDING ORGANIZATIONAL SKILLS

ORGANIZING INFORMATION

In 1988, a famous painting by Manet disappeared from a museum in Huntington, New York. Here is a list of some important facts involved in the case. Put them in the correct chronological order by numbering them from 1 to 6.

_____ The thief confessed to the police that he had stolen the painting and told them that it was in the laundry room of a New York City apartment building.

_____ Two workmen found the painting.

_____ Manet's *Bouquet de Pivoines* was stolen from the Heckscher Museum.

_____ Police located the missing painting.

_____ The building superintendent left the painting in a storage room in the apartment building.

_____ Police searched for the missing painting in the laundry room.

MATCHING

The article mentions several people involved in the recovery of stolen works of art. Match the people in the left column with their opinions in the right column.

NAMES	OPINIONS
_____ Anne Hawley	a. The number of legitimate collectors, dealers, and museums who unknowingly deal in stolen art is surprising.
_____ Huntington Block	b. The recovery rate for important works of art is 50 percent.
_____ Milton Esterow	c. Many art thieves don't realize how difficult it is to sell stolen art.
_____ James D. Keith	d. Some masterpieces are being held by drug dealers.
_____ William E. Martin	e. The punishment for art theft is too mild.

TALK IT OVER

DISCUSSION QUESTIONS

1. Do you agree with Anne Hawley that the punishment for art theft is too mild? Do you know what the punishment is in your country? Is art theft taken seriously in your country? Why or why not?

2. Do you think that it is right or wrong for museums to offer rewards for the recovery of stolen works? What kinds of problems can this lead to?

Read the following selection as quickly as possible and decide which title is the most appropriate. Write the title on the line.

1. Theories and Mysteries in Stone Age Art

2. Cave Art: Good Luck for Hunters

3. Plant-Eaters and Predators

4. Cro-Magnon Hunting Techniques

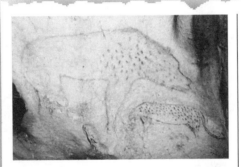

On Christmas Eve in 1994, humans entered a cave in the mountains of southeastern France for what was probably the first time in 20,000 years.[1] The vivid images of more than 300 bears, lions, hyenas, rhinos, and a panther that Jean-Marie Chauvet and his assistants found on the cave walls were like none that they had seen before. Unusual in the Grotte Chauvet, as the cave is now called in honor of its discoverer, are depictions of many carnivores and predators. Other known caves from the same geographical area and time period contain only depictions of plant eaters—animals not dangerous to man.

The paintings in this cave refute the old theory that Cro-Magnon people painted animals that they hunted and then ate. Now many specialists in Paleolithic art believe that cave paintings were not part of a ritual to bring good luck to hunters. They point out that while reindeer made up a major part of their diet, there are no drawings of reindeer. They believe that the animals painted were those central to the symbolic and spiritual life of the times—animals that represented something deep and spiritual to the people.

Scientists are hopeful that Grotte Chauvet will yield new information about the art and lifestyle of Cro-Magnon people. They readily admit, however, that little is understood yet as to the reasons why Ice Age artists created their interesting and detailed paintings. Scientists also wonder why some of the pictures were painted in areas that are so difficult to get to, in caves for example that are 2,400 feet under ground and accessible only by crawling through narrow passageways. As Jean Clotte, an expert in rock paintings said, "One can never guess the real reasons. We can never know, either, whether it was men or women who painted these, or whether the art involved magic or different stages of initiation, or why they chose only to paint the animals and not the flowers or rivers or hillsides around them. Each new discovery sheds a little more light. But it is always like the morning light—it also casts shadows. And because of that, these people will always be somewhat in the mists for us."[2]

WORD FORMS   **A. Complete the chart below by filling in the missing forms of the words.**

VERB	NOUN	ADJECTIVE	ADVERB
	creativity creation	creative	creatively
develop	development	developmental developed developing	
discipline		disciplinary disciplined	
educate	educator education		educationally
experiment		experimental	experimentally
	intelligence		intelligently
intend	intent intention		intentionally
manipulate	manipulator manipulation	manipulative	
	stimulation stimulus stimulant	stimulating stimulated	
visualize	vision visibility visualization		visibly

B. Correct the sentences that have errors in word forms.

1. This product is the result of years of <u>experimental</u>.

2. Aerobic exercise <u>stimulants</u> blood circulation.

3. The right side of the brain controls <u>creative</u> thinking.

4. A baby goes through many <u>developmentally</u> stages in the first three years of life.

5. As I read the travel brochure, I tried to <u>visual</u> the island it was describing.

6. Peter loves to be in control; he tries to <u>manipulative</u> every situation.

7. Perry is very well read and can speak <u>intelligently</u> on a variety of subjects.

8. As an experienced teacher, I question the <u>education</u> objectives of that type of curriculum.

9. I have no <u>intend</u> of helping you with that assignment.

10. Mrs. Tripp is a very strict <u>disciplinarian</u>.

POSTREADING

DISCUSSION
QUESTIONS

1. Jawaharlal Nehru said, "The art of a people is a mirror of their minds. It is a faithful mirror of the life and civilization of a period." Based on your knowledge of history and art, how is this true?

2. Do you agree with poet Henry Wadsworth Longfellow that "Art is power" or with author Oscar Wilde that "All art is quite useless"?

3. Do you think that art can be used as a political tool? In what ways? What examples can you think of?

4. What makes a work of art a masterpiece? In other words, why is some art considered to be great?

5. Art historian Helen Gardner believes "Art is essential to human well-being."[3] She once asked what kind of life would result if the finest of our buildings, pottery, pictures, music, poetry, drama, and dance were taken away? How would you answer this question?

JUST FOR FUN

WORD SCRAMBLE

In groups, unscramble the letters below to spell the names of several well-known artists. Then check your answers on page 229 of the Answer Key.

1. Y A G O

— — —(—)

2. R O L W A H

— — — — — —

3. E E E R R M V

— — — — — — —

4. I S P A C O S

—(—)— — — — —

5. D I N R O

— — — — —

6. R I R N O E

— — —(—)— —

7. S C A T S A T

— — — — — — —

8. L E O G E R C

—(—)— — — — —

9. EMIGOLCHLENA

(_) _ _ _ _ _ _ _ _ _ _ _ _

10. MERDTBRAN

_ _ _ _ _ (_) _ _ _

11. AGGVONH

_ _ (_) _ _ _ _

12. TIMSESA

_ _ _ _ _ (_) _

You will notice that eight of the letters are circled. Write the eight letters on the spaces below:

_ _ _ _ _ _ _ _

Unscramble these letters to spell the name of a person famous in the world of art.

_ _ _ _ _ _ _ _

READER'S JOURNAL

Choose a topic that relates to the readings in this unit and write for about ten to twenty minutes. Consider writing about one of the quotes in this unit or answering one of the discussion questions.

READER'S JOURNAL

Date: _____

_____

_____

_____

_____

_____

_____

_____

_____

_____

_____

_____

_____

_____

_____

_____

_____

_____

_____

_____

_____

_____

_____

THE MARVELS OF MEDICINE

Selections

It is certainly true that if you have your health, you have everything. More and more people are able to enjoy better health and longer lives because of the advances in modern medicine. Through the readings in this unit, you will explore some of the marvels of not-so-modern medicine, look at the use of technology as applied to medicine, and get a glimpse of what the future may hold.

Think about and then discuss the following questions.

1. What do you consider to be the qualities of a good doctor?

2. What are the major illnesses of concern in your country? How are they treated?

3. What do you think are the major differences between Eastern and Western medicines?

4. Have you ever wanted to be a doctor, nurse, therapist, or other kind of health care provider? Does anyone in your family work in the medical field?

With each important discovery—vaccines, X-rays, antibiotics, and vitamin therapy—the practice of medicine has undergone a revolution. But what does the future hold for medicine? Isaac Asimov gives us an overview of the history of medicine and a look at what he sees for the future in **Isaac Asimov's Futureworld: Medicine.**

BEFORE YOU READ

PREREADING QUESTIONS

1. What do you think have been the most important advances in the history of medicine?

2. What advances would you like to see in medicine in the future?

3. Have you ever been hospitalized? For how long? What was it like? How could hospitalization be made better in the future?

Isaac Asimov's Futureworld: Medicine

Computers will diagnose illness.

By Isaac Asimov

1 Everyone agrees that it is safer, easier and cheaper to prevent a disease than to try to cure it.

2 The first great victory in medicine came in 1798, when vaccination was worked out so that smallpox could be prevented.

3 In the 1860's, the germ theory of disease was advanced and doctors began to devise ways of preventing germs from invading the body, and of fighting them once they did.

4 We can handle most germ diseases now, but the great danger to human life and health are the so-called degenerative diseases. Those involve the breakdown of the body machinery, so that a person may come to suffer from cancer, heart trouble, arthritis, diabetes, senility, and so on.

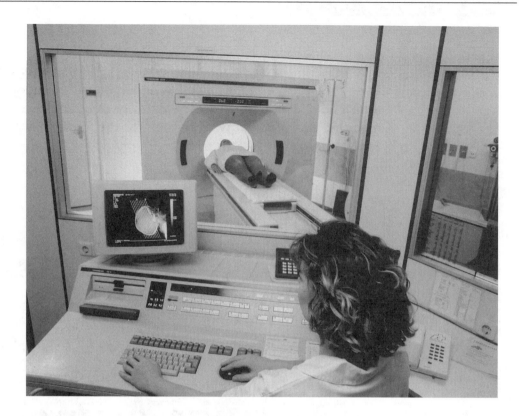

5   The medical profession has learned a great deal about how to organize the way we eat so as to make such diseases less likely. They have learned how to use vitamins and hormones to keep body machinery in better shape.

6   However, do what we may, those degenerative diseases will come eventually, and the body will break down altogether. So in the end, every human being must die. Still, if the diseases are postponed as long as possible, we will all have a stronger and healthier old age. If we must die, let us at least not have a long period of weakness and pain before we go.

7   That means that medical practice of the future will concentrate more and more on diagnosis, or detecting changes in the body at an early stage. Any breakdown is easier to treat if you catch it at the very start, before it has had a chance to establish itself and begin to do much damage.

8   Modern diagnosis began in the 1890's with the discovery of X-rays. For the first time, it became possible to look inside the body without having to cut it. X-rays, however, only detect large atoms. We can see bones clearly, but the soft tissues remain fuzzy. Besides, X-rays are so energetic they can damage the body and even induce cancer.

9   In recent years, however, other methods for viewing the interior of the body have been advanced. We can use very short sound waves (ultrasonic waves) that are much less dangerous than X-rays. Also, something called "magnetic resonance" can detect different atoms by their reaction to a magnetic field—even in soft tissue. It reveals what X-rays do not, and seems to be harmless to the body.

10 We can expect that, in the future, ultrasonic waves, magnetic resonance and, perhaps, other techniques will make it possible to detect anything in the body that is beginning to be abnormal. The analysis of small quantities of blood will be refined so that, again, anything abnormal in it can be picked up.

11 In the future, then, hospitals will be places where one goes primarily for diagnosis. Every human being will "see a hospital" once or twice a year and undergo a rapid and painless analysis of his body structure. The results of the analysis can be compared to those from a year earlier to see what changes have taken place.

12 Nor will doctors have to rely on memory or comparison of written records. It is likely that computers will keep track of a patient and make diagnosis almost as quickly as the body analysis is carried through.

13 The result is that when treatment for disease must be undergone, it will be simpler and take less time. Hospital stays will be greatly reduced and medical expenses will go down.

Dr. Asimov was born in the Soviet Union in 1920. He moved to the United States with his family at age 3. He read his first science fiction story at age 9 and earned his first college degree at 19. By the time the renowned scientist and author died in 1992, he had written more than 500 books.

14 Medical advances will move in even more fundamental directions. The body machinery is directed by the genes, which we inherit from our parents, and which keep reproducing themselves so that they are found in every cell. Sometimes a defective gene is inherited and the body does not function well from birth. Sometimes perfectly useful genes change within the body during a person's lifetime to produce imperfections.

15 It was only in 1953 that scientists discovered the kind of structures the genes have. Ever since, they have been trying to work out the details of each individual gene and studying how they might be transferred from one cell to another, or how they might be changed. This is called "genetic engineering."

16 Certain harmful conditions that a person is born with can be traced back to a particular defective gene. In fact, scientists are planning a huge "genome project" to identify and study the structure of every single gene in the human cells. The time will come when an individual can have his genes mapped and any defective ones may be pinpointed.

17 It is possible that, as techniques improve, every woman who is bearing a child can have its genes tested even before that child is born. Any serious abnormalities will be detected, and some decisions can be made as to what to do.

18 What's more, it may become possible to place a normal gene into cells afflicted with a defective one, or to actually modify the defective gene so as to make it work well. That sort of thing may prove to be our greatest weapon against many diseases.

19 For example, using those techniques, scientists may someday find a cure for cystic fibrosis. That is the most common inherited fatal disease among children in America.

20 As medicine becomes more powerful in the future, however, serious ethical problems may arise. Should parents be able to choose the sex of their children? What if everyone decides they want to have boys?

As medicine becomes more powerful, serious ethical problems may arise.

21 If we can change genes, we will be designing new human beings, so to speak. What kind of human beings do we want? Do we want them all tall

and good-looking? (After all, different people have different ways of considering what is good-looking.) Which is more important, being smart or being kindhearted? Are there genes that encourage a kind heart?

22 Most of all, what if we make it possible for people to live much longer than they do? Won't that mean we must all have fewer children to keep the earth from becoming too crowded?

23 It's important to think about those things—to diagnose the possible ills of society (as well as of human individuals) before they establish themselves and do harm.

• •

BUILDING READING SKILLS

EXAMINING PREDICTIONS

Isaac Asimov wrote this article in 1991, but already several of the predictions have become reality. Read the article carefully and make a list of Asimov's predictions. Then put a check mark next to the ones that have already come true.

_____

_____

_____

_____

_____

_____

_____

_____

EXPANDING VOCABULARY

DEFINING TERMS

Look back through the article and underline each of the following terms. Then, using context from the paragraph cited, write a definition for each one. Do not use your dictionary.

1. germ theory (¶3) _____

_____

2. degenerative disease (¶4) _____

_____

3. X-rays (¶8) _____

_____

4. ultrasonic waves (¶9) _____

_____

5. magnetic resonance (¶9) _____

_____

6. genetic engineering (¶15) _____

_____

7. genome project (¶16) _____

_____

TALK IT OVER

DISCUSSION
QUESTIONS

1. What are some of the problems related to longevity? Do you think that researchers should continue working on ways to prolong life?

2. Name at least three factors, other than medical progress, that contribute to the fact that people live longer now than in the past.

3. Why do you think scientists have not been able to find cures for diseases such as cancer, AIDS, and heart disease?

4. Do you believe that genetic engineering is ethical? Why or why not?

5. Advances in medical science have made possible several controversial procedures, such as organ transplants and in vitro fertilization. Name several other controversial procedures and discuss whether or not you believe they should be used.

FYi

With the help of robots, doctors may soon be able to perform surgery by remote control on patients a thousand miles away. A doctor in New York, for example, may be able to operate on a patient in Antarctica or on a submarine.

A robot is a mechanical device that can perform a wide variety of tasks automatically. Robots are especially useful for doing jobs that are difficult, repetitive, or dangerous. For this reason, they are very adept at assisting in surgery. In **World's First Robot Surgeon Proves a Smooth Operator,** you will read about the many benefits of robotic surgery.

1. What are some uses of robots? What purposes might they serve in the future?

2. Do you think that robots can replace human beings in doing certain jobs? Which ones? What types of jobs will robots never be suited for?

Read the article one time quickly and do the exercise that follows.

World's First Robot Surgeon Proves a Smooth Operator

BY JENNIFER PINKERTON

Surgeons at Johns Hopkins and other hospitals are performing operations with robots that never flinch or fatigue— and don't require years of training.

1   The Johns Hopkins School of Medicine has a new surgical assistant. His name is AESOP, short for Automated Endoscopic System for Optimal Positioning.

2   The world's first robot in the operating room is just an arm—an electronic limb that manipulates instruments (in particular, miniature cameras used during surgery) usually controlled by a human. But unlike a human, AESOP never bumps into anyone, never drops the instruments

and is rock steady. No matter how long the operation, AESOP never tires or suffers from stress.

3   Besides providing the precision required for repetitive actions during surgery, the machine also decreases the risk of infection for patients and doctors. Plus, the robot does not have to undergo years of education: AESOP is inexpensive compared with the cost of training surgical assistants and could "decrease the need for surgeons and surgical specialists," says Dr. Louis Kavoussi, director of the Brady Urological Institute and a surgeon who tested the robot.

4   He and his team at Johns Hopkins Bayview Medical Center have performed several operations using the new robot, exploring how doctors can work together with the new technology: Surgeons watching a monitor in an anteroom directed others working at the operating table. Such procedures hold promise for battlefield and emergency operations in remote areas; surgeons in one part of the world will be able to assist colleagues in another. With AESOP, says Kavoussi, a much-needed specialist "could be in several different hospitals in one day."

5   Robots could revolutionize more conventional procedures as well. In minimally invasive surgery—considered less traumatic for the patient–the surgeon makes small incisions and

Alex Gonzales/Insight

inserts a miniature camera into the patient to view the organs on a monitor—in effect, performing the work by video. But frequent repositioning of the scope stretches out the operation and the time a patient spends under anesthesia, fatiguing all concerned.

6   Robot-assisted surgery, however, features a "ReView" control that allows the surgeon to return to key operative sites or tool-insertion points with a push of a button. Engineers who designed AESOP at Computer Motion Inc. of California are working on several other user-friendly features, as well as a voice-activated robot that would be easier to control and could hold and manipulate tissue.

7   Computer Motion President Yulun Wang and a staff of 29 have worked on AESOP for about three years. It was cleared by the Food and Drug Administration for marketing in December after being tested in 10 hospitals across the country. All of those hospitals have ordered the robot or have orders "in the works," Wang said.

8   Although AESOP in its current version lacks the capacity to make "judgment calls" during surgery, "for a first model, it's very good," says Kavoussi, who already prefers the machine to human assistants. "It's very exciting," he says. "This is the first step in the entry of robotics into the field of medicine."

RECOGNIZING
MAIN IDEAS

Which of the following topics are discussed in the article? Put a check mark next to those topics.

_____ 1. the benefits of using robots in surgery

_____ 2. an explanation of ways that doctors can work with the new technology

_____ 3. a description of how the robot's camera works

_____ 4. the ways AESOP might be improved in the future

_____ 5. the problems associated with using robots to assist surgeons

_____ 6. how robots might help revolutionize conventional procedures

Now read the article again more carefully and do the exercises that follow.

HOW WELL DID
YOU READ?

Answer the following questions.

1. What advantages of AESOP does the author mention? Make a list below.

_____

_____

_____

_____

_____

_____

2. What technological improvements of AESOP are engineers working on?

3. How might robots revolutionize routine surgery?

FYI

China has the largest number of hospitals in the world and the largest number of doctors.

EXPANDING
VOCABULARY

DEFINING TERMS

Choose five words from this article that are new to you and teach them to your classmates. Present a definition for each word and a sentence that uses the word.

1. _____

_____

2. _____

_____

3. _____

_____

4. _____

_____

5. _____

_____

BUILDING WRITING SKILLS

SUMMARIZING

Summarize the main ideas of "World's First Robot Surgeon" on the lines below.

_____
_____
_____
_____
_____
_____
_____
_____

TALK IT OVER

DISCUSSION QUESTIONS

1. Would you prefer to be operated on by a person or a robot? Why?

2. Do you think that technology has dehumanized medicine? In other words, are doctors nowadays paying enough attention to the emotional needs of the patient? Do you think a balance between technology and empathy is possible? Why or why not?

3. How are doctors trained in your country? How long is the training period? What advantages might robots have in this regard? What disadvantages?

4. In the past, a person was declared dead when his or her heart stopped beating. Now, a machine can keep a heart beating. Is this necessarily progress? Why or why not?

Read the following selection as quickly as possible and decide which title is the most appropriate. Write the title on the line.

1. Symptoms of Polio

2. Salk and Sabin: A Bitter Feud

3. Jonas Salk: The Savior of Summer

4. The Spread of Polio

In the childhood of today's 40-somethings and those older, the end of the school year brought not the freedom to frolic in sun and surf, but, for many, strict parental orders to avoid the public pool, the local swimming hole, and that lusciously cool curiosity, the air-conditioned movie house. For summer was the dread polio season. No one knew how paralytic poliomyelitis spread. But everyone assumed that crowds were a good place to get a one-way ticket to an iron lung.* Mothers admonished children to report *immediately* the slightest sore throat or, most feared of all, a stiff neck, and to stick with old friends (whose germs they already had). Yet children—especially children, for reasons no one understood—still caught the sometimes-fatal disease, and the little bodies piled up in hospital wards like driftwood. Front pages reported the weekly toll. There were a record 57,879 cases in 1952, all incurable. In 1954 the National Foundation for Infantile Paralysis, having collected 75 million dimes in theaters throughout the country, funded tests of the first polio vaccine, on 1.8 million schoolchildren. On April 12, 1955, an upstart young researcher announced the results. "The vaccine works," declared Jonas Salk.

Church bells pealed, some schools closed for the day, factories observed a moment of silence. Salk's announcement sparked a tectonic shift in the way people thought and lived.

"There was suddenly a release from this great fear—the dread that occurred each summer." Salk recalled. Within weeks children by the thousands lined up for the shots. The annual number of cases dropped to a dozen or fewer. Now, according to medical experts, the disease has been virtually eradicated in the industrialized world. Salk became a medical legend, an instant hero to millions and the man who gave summertime back to the children.

When Salk died of heart failure at the age of 80 last week in La Jolla, Calif., he had reaped every honor the public and

---

* **Iron lung** A metal machine that fits over the body and helps a person breathe by regulating changes in air pressure.

government could bestow, starting with the Congressional Gold Medal. The oldest son of a garment worker, Salk grew up in a New York City tenement and paid for his education largely through scholarships. But the scientific establishment never embraced Salk. He was never elected to the National Academy of Sciences; academicians sniffed that his work was not "original." All he did was grow the polio virus in monkey kidney cells, they said, which three Harvard biologists discovered how to do (they won the 1954 Nobel Prize for it); then he killed the virus with formaldehyde and injected it into volunteers. Dr. Albert Sabin, a rival in the race for a polio vaccine, derided it as "pure kitchen chemistry." Salk saw it differently. The Harvard team "threw a long forward pass," he said. "I caught it."

Bitter feud: To do that, he had to fight off the defensive backs of scientific orthodoxy. "Dogma held that you couldn't immunize with a killed virus; you had to go through an infection to get immunity," Salk recalled in a 1980 interview. Some virologists argued vehemently that the killed-virus vaccine was inferior and should not be given to the public. Although the 1954 trials proved them wrong, Salk's vaccine was superseded in 1962 by Sabin's oral version. Made with live but weakened viruses, it offers lifetime immunity and is easier to store and administer. The intense, supremely confident Salk feuded bitterly with Sabin, who died in 1993. He delighted in pointing out that live vaccine could, and did, cause polio (though in practice it rarely did).

In his later years Salk became more the speculative scientist-philosopher. He mused that humans could direct their own evolution, and founded the renowned Salk Institute for Biological Studies in La Jolla. Divorced from the mother of his three sons, in 1970 Salk married Picasso's longtime companion, Françoise Gilot. In the 1980s he began a quest for a vaccine that would prevent full-blown AIDS, in people infected with HIV, by boosting their immune system. AIDS scientists scoffed. But "there have to be people who are ahead of their time," Salk said. "That is my fate."

BY SHARON BEGLEY

All over the world, medical practices have been handed down from one generation to the next with almost no change. These practices include both traditional and alternative forms of therapy for conditions ranging from the common cold to cancer. The following article, **Chinese Medicine,** describes one doctor's view of the differences between Chinese and Western Medicine.

BEFORE YOU READ

PREREADING QUESTIONS

1. Do you know anything about Traditional Chinese Medicine? If so, share your information with your classmates.

2. Do you use any special herbs to prevent or cure ailments? What herbs do you use? Where did you learn about their curative powers?

3. Have you ever been to an acupuncturist? If yes, was the treatment successful? If no, would you ever consider trying acupuncture?

Chinese Medicine

BY JOAN GOLDSTEIN

The best Chinese doctors are said to be those whose patients remain healthy.

1   "The main difference between Traditional Chinese Medicine (TCM) and Western medicine is that TCM focuses on health rather than disease," says Qing Cai Zhang, M.D., a private practitioner of TCM in New York City. "It focuses on keeping the body in balance and harmony with nature."

2   In China, the best doctors are said to be those whose patients remain healthy. This is accomplished through supporting the body's natural order (thereby enhancing immunity before imbalance and disease occur) and reducing the potency of pathogens.

3   Observation plays an essential part in the Chinese practitioner's diagnoses, says Dr. Zhang. Everything about the person is observed, from his tongue, eyes, skin color, hearing, pulse, age, weight, and body type to his voice, hair, posture, and body odor.

4   A complete examination of this type reveals potentially weak areas. Herbal formulas are then prescribed to tone these areas as well as to bolster the immune system. (Acupuncture, which is considered a form of physical therapy, is used as an adjunct to herbology.)

5   Herbology is particularly effective at helping to eliminate what the Chinese call "evils": viruses, bacterial infections, or anything else that invades the body from the outside. In the event that evils are present, the doctor prescribes herbs not only for the affected part but to strengthen other parts which may be weakened by the disease. In this way body balance is maintained, and a well-balanced body is thought to heal itself more efficiently.

6   "Allopathy (Western medicine) eliminates evils without supporting the normal order," says Dr. Zhang. It uses the so-called magic-bullet idea: Kill the problem, kill the disease, which can often harm the body. But, says Dr. Zhang, "If you have a mouse in the house you set a mousetrap, you don't burn the house down."

7   Chinese medicine is particularly effective in treating AIDS patients, says Dr. Zhang. The high toxicity of Western AIDS drugs (such as AZT) often damages vital tissues like bone marrow and those lining the gastrointestinal system, further weakening the patient. Zhang claims that some herbs, on the other hand, support or increase the body's natural killer immune cells while leaving the body's vital growth mechanisms intact.

8   Many conventional doctors who treat AIDS patients acknowledge that TCM does have some efficacy. "Traditional Chinese Medicine does offer specific treatments for some of the ailments for which I don't have much to offer," says Bernard Bihari, M.D., associate professor of medicine at the State University of New York Health Science Center in Brooklyn.

9   "For instance, many people with AIDS run constant low-grade fevers and have night sweats, and a combination of Chinese herbs and acupuncture is often very effective at treating these symptoms."

10   But Dr. Bihari is less sure about the power of certain herbs to boost immunity. "Whenever you are testing something, there is often initially a very powerful placebo effect.* Everybody's T cells** go up, whether they're on a placebo or the ingredient being tested," he says.

11   Dr. Zhang stresses that TCM does have its limitations and cautions that some "evils" do require the intervention of Western medicine. Injuries, traumas, and illnesses where time is of the essence definitely call for the "heroic" Western approach. However, says Dr. Zhang, even in these cases, subsequent healing can be enhanced with herbs and acupuncture.

* **Placebo effect** The phenomenon in which people get better because they believe they will. A placebo is a substance given instead of real medicine to reinforce a patient's expectation to get well.
** **T cells** Cells in human blood that function in the development of immunity.

Circle the letter of the choice that best completes the sentence or answers the question.

1. What is the main purpose of the article?

    a. to explain how acupuncture works
    b. to describe the limitations of Traditional Chinese Medicine
    c. to show the differences between Traditional Chinese Medicine and Western medicine
    d. to provide a short history of Traditional Chinese Medicine

2. The phrase *these areas* in paragraph 4 refers to _____.

    a. potentially weak places
    b. herbal formulas
    c. immune systems
    d. acupuncture and herbology

3. The word *potency* in paragraph 2 is closest in meaning to _____.

    a. weakness
    b. balance
    c. penalty
    d. strength

4. The author would support which of the following conclusions?

    a. Allopathy is effective in supporting balance.
    b. Both traditional Chinese and Western approaches have a place in modern medicine.
    c. Herbal formulas are generally the best way to bolster the immune system.
    d. Traditional Chinese Medicine has proven to be very effective in treating injuries and trauma.

5. According to the article, which of the following is an important part of diagnosis in TCM?

    a. allopathy
    b. acupuncture
    c. observation
    d. herbology

6. The word *bolster* in paragraph 4 is closest in meaning to _____.

    a. prescribe
    b. support
    c. discount
    d. fight

7. According to the author, many conventional doctors who treat AIDS patients believe that _____.

    a. TCM can be effective in treating some ailments
    b. there is no place for TCM in Western countries
    c. acupuncture is the best form of physical therapy
    d. AZT has no negative side effects

8. The word *vital* in paragraph 7 is closest in meaning to _____.

    a. extra
    b. powerful
    c. essential
    d. delicate

9. According to the article, which of the following is not true about TCM?

    a. It relies heavily on allopathy.
    b. It tries to maintain the balance of the body.
    c. It uses herbal formulas and acupuncture.
    d. It treats the whole person.

BUILDING READING SKILLS

EXAMINING DIFFERENCES

The author mentions several differences between Traditional Chinese Medicine and Western medicine. Summarize the differences in the boxes below.

Traditional Chinese Medicine	Western Medicine

Read the following excerpt from an encyclopedia article about medicine in China and then list three new facts you learned.

One of the most profound recent changes in health services in China has involved the renewed interest in Traditional Chinese Medicine: local herbal medications, folk medicine, and acupuncture, for example. Such treatment is now more common in China than is Western-style medicine. In communes, as much as four-fifths of the medication utilized may be herbal. A paramedical corps of so-called barefoot doctors plays an important role in bringing health services to the people. These personnel are trained in hygiene, preventive medicine, acupuncture, and routine treatment of common diseases. They operate in rural areas where both Chinese and Western-style doctors are scarce. For millions of peasants the barefoot doctor is their first encounter with anyone trained in health services.[1]

1. _____

   _____

2. _____

   _____

3. _____

   _____

1. How widespread is the use of non-Western medicine in your country? Have you ever tried any type of alternative medicine such as acupuncture?

2. Why does Dr. Zhang use the expressions "magic bullet" and "heroic" to describe the approach of Western medicine?

3. What do you think the advantages and disadvantages of TCM are? What about Western medicine?

4. "In the 1950s and 1960s the focus of care became not the person, but the disease," says Dr. Mack Lipkin. "It also became the approach in medical schools and medical centers. And we're still living with that."[2] Why does this fact bother doctors like Dr. Lipkin?

Read the following selection as quickly as possible and decide which title is the most appropriate. Write the title on the line.

1. Mystical Qualities of the Liver

2. You're Sick? It Depends on Where You're From

3. Medicine in the United Kingdom

4. Antibiotics—The Miracle Drug

Pharmaceutical companies have commissioned a study to help them package and market their products throughout Europe. This is because they know there are deep-rooted national differences in how people think about health, disease, and medicine.

In the United Kingdom and Holland, when taking medicine, people prefer tablets. In France, suppositories are preferred, and in Germany an injection will do.

In different countries, different organs are believed to be the cause of illness. Germans are almost obsessive about the heart and circulation—they are Europe's largest consumers of heart medicine. Southern Europeans assign almost mystical qualities to the liver. In the United States and Britain, doctors tend to look for external agents attacking the body, and they prescribe antibiotics.

In Central European countries, people turn first to herbal treatments and hot and cold baths, relying on antibiotics only as remedies of last resort.

If you say you are tired, Germans would say it is cardiac insufficiency. In England, they would consider you depressed. In the United States, it would be a virus.[3]

The loss of the habitats of many plant and animal species is causing a medical emergency. Many species are dying out before scientists have time to fully explore their medicinal potential. As you read **Frogs and Human Health,** think about how our hopes for finding cures for many of today's killer diseases are vanishing as quickly as some species.

BEFORE YOU READ

PREREADING QUESTIONS

1. What steps are being taken to protect wildlife in your country?

2. Which animals do you think are important to medical research?

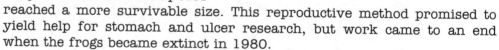

Frogs and Human Health

BY BILL SHARP

1   Queensland breeding frogs in the mountains of Australia protected their young from predation by swallowing the eggs and spitting them out only when the tadpoles reached a more survivable size. This reproductive method promised to yield help for stomach and ulcer research, but work came to an end when the frogs became extinct in 1980.

2   Frogs have devised unique chemical adaptations that make them valuable helpers in the search for new, more effective medicines for ailments such as ulcers, arthritis, burns, cardiac arrhythmia, extreme pain, and neurological diseases such as Alzheimer's, myasthenia gravis, and amyotrophic lateral sclerosis. For example, toads, including the endangered Houston toad, produce alkaloids similar to digitalis that may benefit heart patients. Some of these alkaloids also have pain-killing properties much like morphine.

3   The most medically interesting amphibians found to date are the dart-poison frogs of Central and South America, whose skins excrete a variety of valuable compounds. Unlike aquatic frogs, whose agility allows them to escape quickly to the safety of nearby water, terrestrial frogs have developed chemical defenses, including the ability to render themselves extremely unpalatable through their secretions.

4   Dart-poison frogs are so named because for generations Colombian Indians poisoned the tips of their blow darts with toxins from the skins of these small and often brightly colored forest frogs. John Daly, chief of bio-organic chemistry for the National Institutes of Health (NIH), in Bethesda, Maryland, has studied these and other natural sources of medically useful compounds. Alkaloid compounds found in the skin of these frogs by Daly and others are used as tools worldwide in research on nerve and muscle function, as well as in anti-convulsants and anti-arthritics research.

5   Antibiotic peptides from another frog are the basis of products under development for wound and burn therapy by a former NIH research scientist. Other frog peptides may be useful for studies of appetite and temperature regulation. Another compound isolated from the skin of an Ecuadorian poison frog has 200 times the pain-killing power of morphine. Drugs based on the discovery are under development at several drug companies.

6   Eric Chivian of Physicians for Social Responsibility writes in *Critical Condition: Human Health and the Environment,* "The current loss of biological diversity represents nothing less than a medical emergency, and would demand that efforts to preserve species and ecosystems be given the highest priority."

7   Thomas Eisner, professor of biology at Cornell University, says, "For thirty years I've been doing nothing but searching for chemicals in nature. It makes me very aware of what we don't know. When we lose species, we are destroying our legacy. Our biggest source of biochemical information for the future is what is recorded in nature."

8   Because they are niche species in tropical forests that are dwindling daily, all of the 100 species of dart-poison frogs, along with the information they represent, are today threatened by rain forest destruction.

9   As Eisner and others have noted, when we destroy a species, we are burning an irreplaceable book of information.

BILL SHARP is co-owner of Fresh Air Communications, Newburyport, Massachusetts, a free-lance writing firm specializing in environment, health, and technology topics.

Circle the letter of the choice that best completes the sentence or answers the question.

1. The article mainly discusses _____.

   a. the differences between dart-poison frogs and aquatic frogs
   b. the ways frogs can benefit human health
   c. the reproductive method of frogs
   d. the biological diversity of the rain forest

2. According to the author, frogs are helpful in the development of new medicines because of their _____.

   a. unique chemical adaptations
   b. physical agility
   c. dwindling numbers
   d. reproductive methods

3. According to the article, dart-poison frogs are threatened by which of the following?

   a. toxins from their skins
   b. inability to control their body temperature
   c. biochemical information
   d. destruction of the rain forest

4. It can be inferred from the article that terrestrial frogs are _____.

   a. found mainly in Australia
   b. less interesting to medical researchers than aquatic frogs
   c. becoming extinct more quickly than aquatic frogs
   d. unable to survive on land

5. The word *them* in the second sentence of paragraph 3 refers to _____.

   a. aquatic frogs
   b. terrestrial frogs
   c. toads
   d. dart-poison frogs

6. The word *their* in the first sentence of paragraph 4 refers to _____.

   a. medical researchers
   b. dart-poison frogs
   c. Colombian Indians
   d. Central Americans

7. Where does the author describe the reproductive method of Queensland breeding frogs?

   a. paragraph 1
   b. paragraph 3
   c. paragraph 4
   d. paragraph 7

8. Which of the following is not mentioned as an area of research on alkaloid compounds from frogs and toads?

   a. heart disease
   b. nerve and muscle functions
   c. drug addiction
   d. arthritis

9. The article supports which of the following conclusions?

   a. Niche species in tropical rain forests are valuable resources that need to be protected.
   b. The loss of biological diversity is less important now than it was 50 years ago.
   c. The inability of frogs to adapt to their environment lessens their research value.
   d. Too much time and money is being spent on research into the medical benefits of frogs.

EXPANDING VOCABULARY

A. Answer the following questions with a word from the article.

1. Which word in paragraph 1 means *reproducing*?

   _____

2. Which word in paragraph 3 means *to eliminate from the body*?

   _____

3. Which word in paragraph 3 is used to describe animals that live in the water?

   _____

4. Which word in paragraph 3 is used to describe animals that live on land?

   _____

5. Which word in paragraph 3 means *distasteful*?

   _____

(continued on the next page)

6. Which word in paragraph 4 is a synonym of *poisons*?

   _____

7. Which word in paragraph 5 means *injury*?

   _____

8. Which word in paragraph 6 is an antonym of *destroy*?

   _____

9. Which word in paragraph 7 means *inheritance*?

   _____

10. Which word in paragraph 8 is a synonym for *decreasing*?

   _____

B. Now write a sentence of your own using each of the words.

1. _____
2. _____
3. _____
4. _____
5. _____
6. _____
7. _____
8. _____
9. _____
10. _____

READ AND REACT

1. Make a list of some of the potential benefits that frogs offer the medical world.

   _____

   _____

   _____

   _____

2. Eric Chivian states, "The current loss of biological diversity represents nothing less than a medical emergency, and would demand that efforts to preserve species and ecosystems be given the highest priority." What can we do to improve this situation?

3. Dr. Thomas Eisner says, "For thirty years I've been doing nothing but searching for chemicals in nature. It makes me very aware of what we don't know. When we lose species, we are destroying our legacy. Our biggest source of biochemical information for the future is what is recorded in nature." What exactly does Dr. Eisner mean by this?

4. The last line of the article states, "When we destroy a species, we are burning an irreplaceable book of information." How is this true? What other "irreplaceable books of information" might we be in danger of destroying in our fast-paced, modern lives?

TALK IT OVER

DISCUSSION
QUESTIONS

Write five discussion questions for your classmates to answer based on issues raised in the article. Then discuss the answers in small groups.

1. _____

2. _____

3. _____

4. _____

5. _____

PROVERBS

Read and discuss the following sayings about health. Think of some more to add to the list.

1. Early to bed, early to rise, makes a man healthy, wealthy, and wise.

2. Laughter is the best medicine.

3. An apple a day keeps the doctor away.

4. Feed a cold and starve a fever.

5. Hope deferred makes the heart sick.

6. Time heals all wounds.

7. Pain is temporary; pride is permanent.

8. Physician, heal thyself.

9. Always remember: Mind over matter.

WORD FORMS   **A. Complete the chart with the correct word forms.**

VERB	NOUN	ADJECTIVE	ADVERB
	alternative	alternative alternate	alternatively
analyze	analysis analyst		analytically
benefit		beneficial	beneficially
diagnose	diagnosis		
	immunity immunization	immune	
infect		infectious infected	infectiously
inflame	inflammation		
medicate	medicine medication	medical medicated medicinal	
	symptom		symptomatically
	therapy therapist	therapeutic	

B. Complete the sentences below with words from the chart.

1. The little girl cried so hard that her eyes became _____.

2. If you don't agree with your doctor's _____, you should get a second opinion.

3. Chronic fatigue is often a _____ of depression.

4. Some people drink herbal tea for _____ purposes.

5. This shot will make you _____ to certain tropical diseases.

6. The highway was so crowded that we returned home by an

   _____ route.

7. A good leader _____ the causes of both success and failure.

8. Antibiotics are used to fight _____.

9. After a stressful year at work, his vacation had a _____ effect on his state of mind.

10. Dysfunctional families will often seek the advice of a _____.

POSTREADING

DISCUSSION
QUESTIONS

1. Doctors would prefer that people practice more preventive medicine in their lives. What can we do to take better care of our health?

2. Medical costs have risen sharply in the United States since the 1960s. Is this true in your country? What are some of the reasons for these skyrocketing costs?

3. The mind affects the body in many ways. For example, when people are embarrassed, they often blush, and when they are frightened, they often perspire. What other examples can you think of that prove this point?

4. According to the eighteenth-century French writer Voltaire, "The art of medicine consists of amusing the patient while nature cures the disease." In what ways is that still true today?

5. In your opinion, when does human life begin? When does it end?

Complete the crossword puzzle. Then check your answers on page 229 of the Answer Key.

ACROSS

1. essential
3. identification of the nature and cause of a disease
5. discovered polio vaccine
6. poisonous
8. the _____ theory: theory of disease that was advanced in the 1860s
9. a traditional method of treatment using herbs or flowers to prevent and cure diseases
12. method of blocking pain and restoring balance using needles
15. constant, continuing
16. an approach to medicine that focuses on health rather than disease
17. western medicine
19. length of life
21. injury
22. harm, to damage
23. quantity of medicine that should be taken

DOWN

2. one who can't sleep
4. medicine that destroys harmful bacteria in the body
7. name for type of diseases that involve the breakdown of the body's machinery
10. to force liquid into the body using a needle
11. one who performs surgery
13. something received from one's ancestors
14. to have _____ against a disease is to have protection against it
17. sickness
18. surgeon's assistant
20. living thing that causes infectious diseases in the body

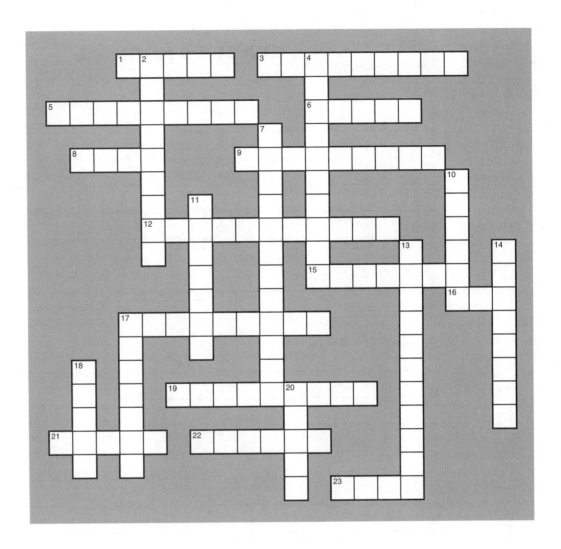

READER'S JOURNAL

Choose a topic that relates to the readings in this unit and write for about ten to twenty minutes. Consider writing about one of the quotes in this unit or answering one of the discussion questions.

READER'S JOURNAL

Date: _____

THE WAY WE ARE

FYi

Unit·5

Selections

As individuals, each and every one of us is unique and special. Yet the characteristics that we have in common are responsible for much of our behavior. In this unit, you will read about some of the interesting areas of human behavior that psychologists are exploring.

Think about and then discuss the following questions.

1. Discuss some of the factors that influence the way you think, behave, and perceive others.

2. Circle the words that best describe you.

cautious	carefree	shy	passive
intellectual	wild	quiet	responsible
upbeat	organized	moody	aggressive
creative	depressed	talkative	determined
humorous	sensitive	social	lethargic
studious	serious	competitive	neurotic
anxious	curious	judgmental	sympathetic
thrifty	ambitious	extravagant	energetic
sarcastic	amiable	patient	ill-tempered
adversarial	witty	antagonistic	perfectionist
rigid	flexible	stylish	conscientious
flirtatious	kind	perky	pessimistic
optimistic	gregarious	spiritual	cynical

3. Why did you circle those words? Give some examples that show why these words describe you.

4. What kind of person are you? Use the space below to write your answer.

_____

_____

_____

_____

_____

It's hard to imagine a world without color. Color brings beauty into our lives and influences the way we behave in many subtle ways. **How Color Can Change Your Life** discusses some of the ways that color affects our lives.

BEFORE YOU READ

PREREADING QUESTIONS

1. In what ways do colors influence your behavior?

2. Do you have a favorite color for clothing? Do you tend to pick the same kinds of colors when you decorate? If so, what are they?

3. Do you prefer to take color or black-and-white photographs? Why?

BUILDING READING SKILLS

PREVIEWING

Before you read the article spend a few minutes previewing it by completing the following steps.

1. Read the title of the article. Think about what it means and try to predict the general topic of the article.

2. Read the headings that are in bold print. Think about how the author might develop the topic. Try to anticipate the kind of information that will be included in each section of the article.

3. Read the first and last paragraph. How is the topic introduced? What conclusions does the author make?

4. Read the first sentence of each paragraph and think about how the article is organized.

5. Put a check mark next to the topics you think might be discussed in the article.

_____ how colors can affect your eating habits

_____ how light is refracted into colors

_____ why countries pick certain colors for their flags

_____ the ways colors can affect your image

_____ how your mood can be influenced by colors

_____ how artists choose colors for their paintings

_____ the relationship between stress and colors

_____ the process of color dying fabrics

_____ how our eyes see color

How Color Can Change Your Life

YOU DON'T HAVE TO BE DOROTHY ENTERING THE LAND OF OZ* FOR THE FIRST TIME TO NOTICE THAT EVERYTHING LOOKS BETTER IN COLOR. BUT BEING AWARE OF COLORS AFFECTS EVERYTHING FROM YOUR MOOD TO YOUR APPETITE. AND ONCE YOU KNOW HOW THEY WORK, YOU CAN MAKE THEM WORK FOR YOU. WE DREW ON THE EXPERTISE OF PSYCHOLOGISTS, BEHAVIORAL SCIENTISTS AND MARKETING RESEARCHERS TO UNCOVER SOME USEFUL NEWS ABOUT HUES.

BY PAMELA STOCK

1 You've been in the office all day. Your brain feels deep-fried. You can barely keep your eyes open. There could be a simple explanation for your dipping energy level—not enough bold blue in your life. A study conducted by the University of California at Berkeley showed that prison guards could consistently lift weights longer when facing a blue poster board than when facing a pink one. So rev up your office walls with artwork that features lots of bright blue: it could help you stay charged if you have to work late. And they might come in handy for an evening softball game—scientists at the University of Texas at Austin found that gazing at a blue light improved athletes' hand-eye coordination.

BEATING STRESS

2 If it's 2 A.M. and you're still tossing and turning over things that happened at work, think pastels. Pink and light blue walls have been shown to lower blood pressure and pulse rates, says health writer Morton Walker, author of *The Power of Color* (Avery, 1990). By hanging up pink or pale blue curtains, you can give yourself a dose of instant calm.

3 Pastels have not cornered the comfort field, however, and if you're feeling stressed to the max, you may find yourself veering to shades of green. Because it is the easiest color for the eye to process, people who are experiencing upheaval in their lives often choose green accessories or housewares, says Cynthia Cornell, the projects coordinator for the Santa Barbara, California-based Wagner Institute for Color Research, a marketing research firm that tracks color trends and performs studies for corporate clients such as Sears, Ford, and Pratt and Lambert Paint. "Those who are drawn to green are often in search of security," she says. Think of it this way—a forest-green throw pillow is a quick, inexpensive and attractive fix.

* **Dorothy entering the Land of Oz** Refers to the popular movie *The Wizard of Oz*, in which Dorothy, a little girl from Kansas, is whisked away by a tornado to a beautiful, mythical land called Oz. In the film, the Kansas scenes are in black and white. When Dorothy lands in Oz, the film suddenly turns into glorious full color.

THE LITTLE BLACK BOX

Black, that wardrobe mainstay is technically not a color at all, but the absorption of all other colors. Culturally, it's long been associated with mourning and depression. An entire office—or as in the case of New York, a whole city—of people wearing black "seems really very sad" says Walker.

People who gravitate to black may be unconsciously unhappy or they could be trying not to be noticed, Walker suggests. Or they could simply be practical and stylish. As Cynthia Cornell advises, "It's important to wear colors you feel comfortable in. We all like black—it makes us feel slender."

EATING WELL

4 If you're munching on everything in sight and even the linoleum is starting to look tempting, you should be on the alert—red alert, that is. The color red has been proven to be a stimulant that releases adrenaline, increases the pulse rate, raises blood pressure and enhances appetite, says Walker. Some fast-food restaurants count on bright red walls to encourage speedy eating and ensure a rapid turnover, according to Cornell.

5 If you're having trouble sticking to a diet, you may want to pick a blue color scheme. Research shows that blue reduces appetite, possibly because so few blue foods exist in nature, suggests Walker. Then again, the key may be cultural—market research reveals that people associate blue (and green) with mold.

GETTING PROMOTED

6 You're excited about starting a new job, and you've decided that your bright red suit will get you noticed. Hold off. You might not be sending the proper message. While small doses of red—such as a scarf or blouse—can be warm and inviting, too much can be overwhelming. And as anyone who's walked through Amsterdam's red-light district knows, the color red screams sex. Instead, go for blue. In the United States, dark blue has historically been associated with power, responsibility and respectability.

7 For contrast, you might give your wardrobe a jolt of yellow. This is the first color that your eye processes, color researchers have discovered, which is why stores use yellow signs to mark sale items. But yellow, like red, is best in small doses—too much has been shown to make people irritable.

8 Keep in mind that color awareness won't make you master of the universe. And you certainly shouldn't feel you have to give up your personal preferences in order to become a savvy color strategist. But color *can* make a difference—in the end, remember, it was the power of Dorothy's ruby slippers** that brought her home safely... even if life in Kansas did turn out to be black-and-white.

** **Dorothy's ruby slippers** In *The Wizard of Oz*, Dorothy wears magical shoes that help her return home to Kansas.

Answer the following questions.

1. What color enhances the appetite? Why?

2. What color is the easiest for the eye to process?

3. What color do stores use to indicate sale items? Why?

4. What color reduces the appetite? Why?

5. How should you use red in your wardrobe for work?

6. What is the color dark-blue associated with in the United States?

**BUILDING
READING SKILLS**

UNDERSTANDING
POINT OF VIEW

Put a check mark next to the statements you think the author would agree with.

_____ 1. A red suit with a blue tie would be a better choice for a job interview than a blue suit with a red tie.

_____ 2. If your job is very stressful, light blue would be a good color to choose for your walls.

_____ 3. Pastels are the only colors that are comforting.

_____ 4. The colors you wear can send important messages to others.

_____ 5. If you want to lose weight, it would not be a good idea to use a lot of red when you decorate your kitchen.

_____ 6. If you have trouble staying awake and concentrating on your work, try moving to a place with lots of bright blue.

_____ 7. Color awareness is the most important ingredient for success on the job.

**BUILDING
READING SKILLS**

SUMMARIZING

In your own words, summarize the main ideas of "How Color Can Change Your Life."

_____

_____

_____

_____

_____

FIGURE IT OUT

COLOR IDIOMS

Write a definition for the italicized idioms in the following sentences. Use the context of the sentences to help you figure out the meanings. Then check your definition with a dictionary or your teacher.

1. After staying inside and studying for final exams for three weeks, we decided to go out and *paint the town red* when our last exam was over.

   _____

2. We *rolled out the red carpet* for the president of our college when he came to our house for dinner.

   _____

3. I can't go to the movies with you tonight. I'm so broke I don't have a *red cent* to my name.

   _____

4. The story about the bank president's stealing money was a *red herring* to turn his employees against him.

   _____

5. It was a *red-letter day* for Carmen when she won the poetry contest.

   _____

6. It took me weeks to change my visa status because there was so much *red tape* involved in the process.

   _____

7. Radio is not as popular now as it was in the past. Nowadays, many radio stations operate *in the red* and, unfortunately, may have to stop broadcasting.

   _____

8. Paul is never satisfied where he is working. He keeps changing his job because, to him, the grass is *always greener on the other side of the fence.*

   _____

(continued on the next page)

115

9. After a fast and scary ride on a roller coaster, all of the children came home looking *green around the gills.*

_____

10. Alice was *green with envy* when she saw her best friend's beautiful engagement ring.

_____

11. My grandmother always has the most beautiful garden in town. Everyone says she has a *green thumb.*

_____

12. The first time Ben went skate boarding he fell so many times that he came home *black and blue.*

_____

13. All businesses try to be *in the black* at the end of the year.

_____

14. Although Dave didn't like his wife's new haircut, he told a *little white lie* and said that he loved it.

_____

15. I usually buy new bed sheets, pillowcases, and towels at the January *white sale.*

_____

16. We're having a hard time selling our grandparent's old house because it's run down and in a dangerous neighborhood. It's a *white elephant.*

_____

17. Antonio argued with his parents until he was *blue in the face,* but they still wouldn't let him borrow their car for the weekend.

_____

18. It was a *blue Monday,* and the students had a hard time staying awake in class after having had so much fun during the weekend.

———————————————————————————————————————

19. Pete is so *yellow-bellied* that he avoids anything that takes courage.

———————————————————————————————————————

20. Yumi started a new routine of exercising daily and eating nutritious food. After a few weeks she felt *in the pink.*

———————————————————————————————————————

21. Nadya was *tickled pink* when her boyfriend gave her a gold necklace for Valentine's Day.

———————————————————————————————————————

TALK IT OVER

DISCUSSION
QUESTIONS

1. The way we feel about different colors is influenced by our culture. What do each of the following colors mean in your culture?

white	blue
black	green
red	yellow

2. Do you have any idiomatic expressions related to color in your language? If so, give some examples.

Read the following selection as quickly as possible and decide which title is the most appropriate. Write the title on the line.

1. A Discovery at the University of Chicago

2. Conversational Distances

3. Pupil Response: A Sensitive Indicator

4. The Advantages of Wearing Dark Glasses

A psychologist at the University of Chicago discovered that the pupil is a very sensitive indicator of how people respond to a situation. When you are interested in something, your pupils dilate; if something is said that you don't like, your pupils would tend to contract. Arabs have known about the pupil response for hundreds, if not thousands, of years. Because people can't control the responses of their eyes, which are a dead giveaway to their mood, many Arabs wear dark glasses, even indoors.

In conversations, Arabs may watch the other person's pupils to judge his or her responses to different topics. By watching the pupils, they can respond rapidly to mood changes. They are adept at reading personal reactions on a second-to-second basis. That's one of the reasons they use a closer conversational distance than North Americans do. At about five feet, the normal distance between two Americans who are talking, it is hard to follow eye movement. But if you use Arab conversational distance, about two feet, you can watch the pupil of the eye.

Direct eye contact for an American is difficult to achieve since Americans are taught not to stare, not to look at the eyes that carefully. If you stare at someone, it is too intense, too sexy, too hostile. It may also mean that, as a group, we are not totally tuned in to our personal interactions. Maybe we should all wear dark glasses.

How good are you at handling stress? Humor is one of the best defenses we have against the stress, emotional isolation, and sense of powerlessness that we all feel at one time or another. As you read **Smile If You're Feeling Stressed,** think about the ways that you deal with tension in your life.

BEFORE YOU READ

PREREADING QUESTIONS

1. Make a list of the kinds of things that stress you the most. Then share your list with your classmates.

   _____

   _____

   _____

   _____

   _____

   _____

2. Discuss some of the best ways you know of to deal with the various kinds of stress in your life.

● ●

Smile If You're Feeling Stressed

HUMOR IS SOMETHING THAT IN THE PAST WAS A CRISIS, BUT IN THE PRESENT IS FUNNY. — CAROL BURNETT

BY BRENDA SHOSS

Laughter: The Great Physician

1   Anyone who has experienced a gut-busting laugh knows how it interrupts tension. Yet many believe they have to trudge to their serious jobs only to come home to deal seriously with their families. Time out! Where do we get the idea that bosses, kids and spouse won't respect us if we lighten up a little?

2   "Humor is something that in the past was a crisis, but in the present is funny," says comedienne Carol Burnett. In all relationships, at work or home, humor lets people put stressful events in perspective.

3   Even large corporations take humor seriously. In a study conducted by Accountemps, 96 percent of executives surveyed think that workers with a sense of humor perform better than those with little or no sense of humor.

4   Laughter also provides physical release from stress. When people laugh, they take deeper breaths. More oxygen means better circulation. Recent studies link laughter to the body's ability to heal. In the book *Anatomy of an Illness,* Norman Cousins cites humor as a way to strengthen the body's own immune system.

5   To date, no one has proved that laughter pills can cure physical problems such as hardening of the arteries. Yet according to Oregon humor writer Jann Mitchell, humor does "stop a hardening of the attitudes in all types of relationships." It is an inexpensive, readily available way to cope with stress.

Types of Goofball Bonding

6   Relationships get into ruts when people forget how to laugh and play. Boring routines, such as housework, can become a source of anger and resentment when couples disagree on who is doing their equal share. Housework takes on a new look when couples wear costumes and scrub to fun music.

7   Humor also brings people together because it is universal. "Laughter is the cement that bonds the group, family or relationship together," say Terry Kellogg and Marvel Harrison in their book, *Finding Balance: 12 Priorities for Interdependence and Joyful Living.* People rarely see things the same way. That's where humor steps in. When two angry people crack up over the same joke, they share a moment of equality. They see each other in a friendlier light.

8   Los Angeles resident John Rennar and his dad frequently travel on business together. While making a hasty exit from a motel parking lot, John drove over what he thought was a speed bump. That bump turned out to be his father's briefcase. Father and son still laugh about the mangled piece of luggage. As a tribute, John's dad created the "Battered Briefcase Award," which he presents annually to the sales rep who commits the most featherbrained act while on the job.

Laugh Off Tension at Work

9   "Too many people view their jobs as a five-day prison from which they are paroled every Friday," says Joel Goodman, founder of The

Humor Project, a humor-consulting group in Saratoga Springs, N.Y. Humor unlocks the office prison because it lets adults bring some of their childlike spirit to the job.

10   According to Howard Pollio, professor of psychology at the University of Tennessee, Knoxville, an office with "humor breaks" is an office with satisfied and productive employees. Pollio conducted a study that proved humor can help workers excel at routine production tasks. Employees perform better when they have fun.

11   In large corporations with a hierarchy of power, there is often no outlet for stress. "Every company needs underground ways of poking fun at the organization," says Lynn M. Mark, a speaker on workplace humor for St. Mary's Health Center in St. Louis.

12   Kodak's Rochester, N.Y., branch discovered a way for its 20,000 employees to uncork their bottled-up resentments. Their 1,000-square-foot "Humor Room" features a "toy store." Among the room's many stress-reducing gadgets, the main attraction is a boss doll with Velcro arms and legs. Employees can dismantle the boss, as long as they put its arms and legs back in place.

13   Every April Fool's day, Sun Microsystems of Mountain View, Calif., concocts an intricate hoax aimed at one of its employees. One year, CEO Scott McNealy's office was decorated as a one-hole, par-four miniature golf course. The annual gag does so much for encouraging teamwork and boosting morale that the company has set aside an April Fool's hoax budget.

14   Sandy Cohen, owner of a graphic print-production business, created "The Quote Board" to document the bizarre phrases people say when under strict deadlines. "When you're under stress, you say stupid things," says Cohen. "Now we just look at each other and say, 'That's one for the Quote Board!'"

Jump on the Laugh Track

15   At work or home, the basic tenet for humor is: Take your responsibilities seriously, but don't take yourself so seriously.

- Figure out what makes you grin. To find your funny bone, start a humor file. Write down jokes, cartoons and real-life situations that are a personal hoot. After a while, you'll learn to recognize your own brand of silliness.

- Plan play time. A pet can be a great spontaneous playmate. "After a stressful day, I play with my dog, Charlie. Soon, I'm talking in goofy voices and laughing like a kid," says Samantha from Boston.
    For those who are not quite sure what "play time" means, try these suggestions: Keep a box of crayons on hand. Go to a comedy club instead of a movie. Dance in your living room to your favorite music. Try a new sport. Red-ink a big "me" on your calendar page to remind yourself to schedule play time.

- Adults in toyland. Toys remind grownups that they are still part kid. Mitchell, the Oregon humorist, surrounds herself with toys at the office and at home. When Mitchell has trouble thinking at work, she dons a gold plastic crown. She then parades around her office until a fresh idea hits her.

Giggles on the Road

16   Psychologist Beth Rom-Rymer agrees that laughter is a way to relieve stress—even in your car. She suggests that strained drivers pop a comedy cassette into their car's tape deck when they're stuck in irritating traffic snarls. Instead of listening to those same old radio commercials, try the humor of Bill Cosby or Jerry Seinfeld to relieve a little tension. Don't laugh too hard, though. The driver in front of you might not see the humor in a rear-end collision!

● ●

HOW WELL DID YOU READ?

Read the following statements. If a statement is true, write *T* on the line. If it is false, write *F*.

_____ 1. Humor helps people put stressful events in perspective.

_____ 2. Large corporations do not take humor seriously.

_____ 3. Laughter provides a physical release from stress.

_____ 4. Humor can help keep relationships exciting.

_____ 5. There is no place for humor in the workplace.

BUILDING READING SKILLS

EXAMINING SUPPORT

The author mentions several areas of life in which humor can be helpful. List them below and explain how humor helps relieve stress in each area.

a. _____

_____

b. _____

_____

c. _____

_____

d. _____

_____

e. _____

_____

FYI

Twenty seconds of hearty laughter gives the body the same kind of workout as three minutes of vigorous exercise. Typically, blood pressure drops and muscles relax.

EXPANDING VOCABULARY

SYNONYMS OR ANTONYMS

Decide if the following pairs of words are synonyms or antonyms. If they are synonyms, circle the *S*. If they are antonyms, circle the *A*.

1. grin	frown	S	A
2. tension	stress	S	A
3. mangled	battered	S	A
4. gag	joke	S	A
5. bizarre	strange	S	A
6. spontaneous	planned	S	A
7. giggle	laugh	S	A
8. hasty	leisurely	S	A
9. irritating	unpleasant	S	A
10. dons	puts on	S	A

READ AND REACT

Discuss the following quotes from the article with your classmates. Then choose one and describe a personal story that proves its truth for you.

1. *Humor is something that in the past was a crisis, but in the present is funny.*

2. *Humor also brings people together because it is universal.*

3. *Laughter is the cement that bonds the group, family or relationship together.*

4. *Every company needs underground ways of poking fun at the organization.*

5. *At work or home, the basic tenet for humor is: Take your responsibilities seriously, but don't take yourself too seriously.*

TALK IT OVER

DISCUSSION QUESTIONS

Read and discuss the following statements.

1. Humor does not translate well. It is the first thing that gets lost in a foreign language.

2. Humor breaks down emotional boundaries.

3. If you don't have a sense of humor, you probably don't have any sense at all.

Aging is the process of growing old. For most of us, the process of aging begins sometime between the ages of thirty and forty. Heredity and environment both play a role in the way that we age. **Brain Power's Sliding Scale** and its sidebar "Use It or Lose It?" present research into the process of aging and examine how it may work differently in men and women.

BEFORE YOU READ

PREREADING ACTIVITY

Read the statements below and decide whether you agree or disagree with each one. Discuss your opinions with your classmates.

1. Women are generally better at verbal skills.

2. The brains of men and women are anatomically different.

3. There are dramatic differences between the way male and female brains age.

4. Older people have a greater range of intellectual ability than younger people.

5. Women's spatial skills start to decline before men's.

• • • • • • • • • • • • • • •

Paul Spiers and Gail Hochanadel, a husband and wife team in Topsfield, are among researchers who have found subtle differences between the mental abilities of men and women as they age.

Brain Power's Sliding Scale

Aging

By Judy Foreman

"Most of the data I have looked at don't show dramatic differences between men and women. They are there, and they are real, but relative to the impact of other things, they are fairly small."

Richard Mohs
Psychologist, Bronx Veterans Affairs Medical Center

1   You would think Harvard psychologist Douglas Powell, 60, would be the last to worry that he was "losing it."

2   After all, he has spent years concocting tests to see which skills—such as attention, visuospatial ability, verbal fluency and memory—slip most with normal aging.

3   In fact, Powell is writing a book on normally aging minds and runs a company that helps hospitals determine if the minds of their oldest doctors are still intact.

4   Yet one day recently, right after being interviewed about mental aging, Powell stopped to put gas in his car and left the gas cap on the trunk. A clear sign, or so he says, of attention deficit, a particular plague for aging men.

5   When he got home, a rattled Powell told his wife Virginia, "I am a wreck. I was talking to the *Globe* about what you lose. This is the second time in a row I've lost the gas cap on the trunk of my car. I'm really losing it."

6   Virginia, also 60 and CEO of their consulting company, was unfazed, noting in wifely fashion that in some ways—like searching for the glasses on top of his head—he had always been this way.

7   It is but small comfort, Powell says, that, in lockstep with his attentional abilities, his wife's map-reading skills have also declined, as visuospatial skills of older women often do.

8   With the passing years, Powell, like many of the rest of us, finds himself ever quicker to pounce on evidence of

mental slippage. And like many a couple, the Powells sometimes think they see gender differences in the foibles of aging minds.

9   But whether such differences in fact exist, and how important they may be, are very much open questions, questions often pursued, curiously enough, by husband-and-wife research teams.

10   The bottom line is that even where gender differences in cognitive aging exist, the effects are probably small. Education, for instance, is by far a more powerful predictor of mental function in later life, notes Richard Mohs, a psychologist at the Bronx Veterans Affairs Medical Center who studies aging and memory as part of a $25 million effort by the Charles A. Dana Foundation in New York.

11   "Most of the data sets I have looked at don't show dramatic differences between men and women," Mohs says. "They are there, and they are real, but relative to the impact of other things, they are fairly small."

12   Still, the more researchers wade into the intellectual—and often political—swamp of gender differences, the more they find small differences in the way male and female brains age.

13   In studies of 200 men and women aged 30 to 80, for instance, Dr. Marilyn Albert, director of gerontology research at Massachusetts General Hospital, has found that women decline faster than men at some spatial tasks, though she stresses that far more noticeable are changes in memory, "executive functions" like planning and problem-solving, and recalling names. All those abilities decline with age in both sexes at the same rate.

14   At Pennsylvania State University, K. Warner Schaie and his wife Sherry Willis, both professors of human development, have studied about 5,000 people—some of them for as long as 35 years—through the Seattle Longitudinal Study, a project Schaie started in 1956 at the University of Washington.

15   Overall, they find, men lose mental skills faster than women, perhaps because at any given age, as Schaie put it in a telephone interview, men are "closer to death."

16   But for many men, skills such as spatial orientation, which is often seen as a male strength, hold up well into the 80s.

17   By contrast, he says, women's spatial ability—often seen as a comparative weakness—declines about twice as much as men's.

18   Schaie, who defines spatial skills as being able to do such things as look at a map and determine which way to turn, or to assemble furniture that comes in pieces, discussed such gender differences in an April article in the *American Psychologist*.

19   Men and women, he finds, decline at about the same rate on inductive reasoning, when tested on such tasks as figuring out the underlying principle in railroad schedules (for example, that a train leaves every hour at 17 minutes past the hour). But because women start out better, they tend to keep this edge into late life, Schaie says.

20   Women also maintain a lifelong advantage at verbal comprehension (recognizing vocabulary), verbal memory (recalling lists of words) and word fluency (generating lists of words that start with a certain letter, for instance).

21   For both men and women, Schaie emphasizes, the most striking thing about aging minds is that the range of intellectual ability is greater among older people than among younger

ones. And for both sexes, he adds, the rule of thumb is that people retain the skills they use in daily life and tend to lose the ones they do not practice. "And in reality," he says, "you can't practice everything."

22   Verbal skills are often well-maintained precisely because most people keep using them, he says, though even for women verbal comprehension declines in the 80s, probably because by this age women are widowed and have less opportunity to talk to someone.

23   Like other researchers, Douglas Powell has found that although women's spatial skills start to slide before men's, both sexes lose mental skills in a distinct order: visuospatial first, then reasoning , then verbal memory. Along with Sandra Weintraub, head of neuropsychology at Beth Israel Hospital, Powell has studied 1,000 physicians, most of them men age 25 to 60, and 600 other men and women.

24   Gail Hochanadel, a psychologist who works with her husband, Paul Spiers, at Neuropsychology Associates in Topsfield, has studied 42 volunteers from the Framingham Heart Study, looking not just at overall test scores but at the kinds of errors that were made.

25   "The type of error can tell us what area of the brain is involved, not just whether performance is impaired," she says.

26   Her error analysis showed that both men and women suffer age-related declines in frontal lobe function, the area of the brain important for "executive" duties such as planning and juggling tasks that have to be done at the same time.

27   But while men's decline begins in the 70s, she finds, "women didn't show it until their 80s."

28   Unlike some researchers, Hochanadel also finds that in their 70s, men also begin to show more errors in right hemisphere function, where spatial tasks are performed. Perhaps, she speculates, the decline in levels of the male hormone, testosterone, in aging men may trigger a decline in spatial abilities.

29   (While there is little data on male hormones and brain function, growing but still-inconclusive data suggest that in women, taking the female hormone estrogen after menopause reduces the risk of Alzheimer's and boosts verbal memory.)

30   Edith Kaplan, associate professor of neurology and psychiatry at Boston University School of Medicine, offers an explanation of the relative mental losses in men and women.

31   Throughout life, she says, men's and women's brains are anatomically different, with women having a thicker *corpus callosum*—a network of fibers—connecting the two hemispheres.

32   Because of the interconnections, she says, it may be easier for women to use their still-strong verbal skills to compensate for declining visuospatial skills.

33   But there is, Kaplan adds, one tactic both sexes can easily use to stay sharp: social interaction, which, research suggests, can help keep a number of cognitive skills intact.

34   Hochanadel strongly agrees: "Party on! It's good for you."

JUDY FORMAN is a member of the Boston Globe staff.

USE IT OR LOSE IT?

Researchers disagree whether the "use it or lose it" philosophy holds for cognitive aging, but there is some evidence that keeping mentally active can slow age-related declines.

At Pennsylvania State University, Sherry Willis and her husband, K. Warner Schaie, have studied 5,000 people, some since 1956. People lucky enough to avoid chronic diseases may also fare better in intellectual function, they find, perhaps because chronic diseases can restrict lifestyle and reduce mental stimulation. Similarly, those lucky enough to be relatively affluent also fare better, perhaps because money can buy intellectually stimulating things like travel.

Education helps, too, researchers say, perhaps because it instills the conviction that you can always learn something new. The Schaie-Willis team also has some other observations. Being in a stable marriage with a stimulating spouse, they say, helps maintain intellectual vigor.

Flexibility counts, too. People who stay mentally vibrant are often those who do not insist that "they must do things today as they did before," Schaie says. In neuropsychological terms, the ability to see problems in new ways often yields higher scores on tests of mental function. And people satisfied with life also stay more mentally fit, he says.

If you find your mental skills sagging, consider working on specific deficits. When Willis gave 5-hour tutorials on inductive reasoning or spatial skills to about 200 people whose skills had declined in the previous 14 years, 40 percent regained lost abilities. That advantage held up seven years later when they were re-tested.

Other ways to stay sharp, Schaie says, are doing jigsaw puzzles to hone visuo-spatial skills, working crossword puzzles for verbal skills, playing bridge for memory and simply matching wits at home with players on TV game shows.

Finally, remember this. Even though you may lose some mental skills with normal aging, you also gain in one key area: wisdom.

At Harvard Medical School, Dr. Marsel Mesulam and Changiz Geula speculate that the growth in wisdom—loosely defined as the maturation of intellectual abilities that comes with life experience—may be linked to the fact that nerve fibers in the brain's association cortex, which integrates different forms of knowledge, continue to be newly myelinated throughout the 40s, 50s and even 60s. Myelination is the process by which nerves are covered with a protective coating, which speeds up neural communication.

The Harvard team has also found that, unlike some other brain chemicals, one called AChE (acetylcholinesterase) continues to be made late in adult life in the "pyramidal" neurons in the cortex, or outer layers of the brain. High levels of AChE in these cells, they speculate, may be associated with the increasing wisdom in later life.

—By Judy Foreman

EVALUATING YOUR OPINIONS Look back at the statements in the prereading section on page 124. Have any of your opinions changed since you read "Brain Power's Sliding Scale"? If so, which ones?

HOW WELL DID YOU READ? Answer the following questions based on information from the article and its sidebar.

1. As people grow older, what kinds of skills do they usually retain? Give a specific example to support your answer.

_____

_____

_____

2. In what order do both sexes lose their mental skills?

_____

_____

3. What is one reason that women may be able to use their strong verbal skills to compensate for declining visuospatial skills as they grow older?

_____

_____

_____

4. According to researchers, what factors help prevent age-related mental decline.

_____

_____

_____

5. What are some examples of specific activities that can help prevent mental decline?

_____

_____

_____

BUILDING READING SKILLS

FACT VERSUS THEORY

Read the following statements. If according to the article a statement is a fact (something that has been proven), write FACT on the line. If according to the article a statement is a theory (someone's idea or assumption that has not yet been proven), write THEORY on the line.

_____ 1. Keeping mentally active can slow age-related mental declines.

_____ 2. Nerve fibers in the association cortex of the brain continue to be myelinated throughout middle age.

_____ 3. Being in a stable marriage with a stimulating spouse helps maintain intellectual functioning.

_____ 4. The brains of men and women are anatomically different.

_____ 5. There are definite, but small, gender differences in the way brains age.

_____ 6. Education, chronic illness, and standard of living all affect cognitive aging.

_____ 7. The frontal lobe of the brain manages tasks that have to be done at the same time.

EXPANDING VOCABULARY

DEFINING TERMS

Look back through the article and underline each of the following terms. Then, using context from the paragraph, write a definition or give examples for each one. Do not use your dictionary.

1. executive functions (¶13) _____

_____

2. spatial skills (¶18) _____

_____

3. inductive reasoning (¶19) _____

_____

4. verbal comprehension (¶ 20) _____

_____

5. verbal memory (¶20) _____

_____

6. word fluency (¶20) _____

_____

7. frontal lobe functions (¶26) _____

_____

8. right hemisphere functions (¶28) _____

_____

9. corpus collosum (¶31) _____

_____

FIGURE IT OUT

IDIOMS

Look back through the article and underline each of the following idiomatic expressions. Then, using context from the paragraph and the sentences provided, write a definition for each one. Finally, write your own sentence that expresses the meaning of the idiom.

1. in a row (¶5)

I'm sure I'll get a good grade in this course. I've gotten As on the last three tests in a row.

definition: _____

sentence: _____

2. the bottom line (¶10)

Jason is having a lot of trouble in his calculus course. Although he is trying very hard, the bottom line is that he needs private tutoring.

definition: _____

sentence: _____

(continued on the next page)

3. put it (¶15)

Madeline put it so well when she said that laughter is the best medicine.

definition: _____

sentence: _____

4. hold up (¶16)

Our good luck held up for the whole season, and we won every soccer game.

definition: _____

sentence: _____

5. figure out (¶19)

Karen couldn't figure out how to use her new computer program.

definition: _____

sentence: _____

6. rule of thumb (¶21)

As a rule of thumb, you should drink lots of liquids on hot days.

definition: _____

sentence: _____

BUILDING WRITING SKILLS

PARAPHRASING

Rewrite the sentences below using your own words. Your sentences should express the main idea of the original sentences as clearly and simply as possible.

1. *With the passing years, Powell, like many of the rest of us, finds himself ever quicker to pounce on evidence of mental slippage.*

_____

_____

2. *Still, the more researchers wade into the intellectual—and often political—swamp of gender differences, the more they find small differences in the way male and female brains age.*

_____

_____

3. *For many men, skills such as spatial orientation, which is often seen as a male strength, hold up well into the 80s.*

_____

_____

4. *For both sexes, … the rule of thumb is that people retain the skills they use in daily life and tend to lose the ones they do not practice.*

_____

_____

PROVERBS

Read and discuss the following sayings about aging. Think of some more to add to the list.

1. Better to wear out than to rust out.

2. You are never too old to learn.

3. They that live longest, see the most.

4. Young folks think that old folks are fools.

5. Youth is wasted on the young.

6. You're only as old as you feel.

_____

_____

_____

_____

Recent research indicates that age, culture, motivation, and gender, as well as hard wiring in the brain, affect the way we think. Read **What Sex Is Your Brain?** and take the quiz to understand more about the way you think.

Complete the following sentences. Then compare your answers with those of your classmates.

1. The way men think is more _____ than the way women think.

2. The way women think is more _____ than the way men think.

3. Men are usually better at _____ , _____ ,

   and _____ than women are.

4. Women are usually better at _____ , _____ ,

   and _____ than men are.

What Sex Is Your Brain?

BY ANNE MOIR AND
DAVID JESSEL

1 "Why can't a woman be more like a man?" goes the exasperated lament. Science is searching for an answer, and researchers have presented some intriguing possibilities. Men and women are different, they theorize, because the slight differences in the way their brains are constructed lead the sexes to process information in subtly different ways.

2 That might be why men generally do better than women in tests of spatial ability—being able to picture objects' shapes, positions and proportions accurately in the mind's eye. Similarly, boys tend to outperform girls in mathematics involving abstract concepts of space, relationships and theory.

3 On the other hand, girls usually say their first words and learn to speak in sentences earlier than boys. Some studies have found that women speak in longer, more complex sentences than men. Also, boys outnumber girls in remedial reading classes. Stuttering and other speech defects occur more frequently among males.

4 What are the anatomical differences in the brains of men and women that might cause these variations? In tests on brains obtained after autopsy, some researchers have found that in women part of the corpus callosum, the bundle of fibers linking the left and right hemispheres, is bigger in relation to overall brain weight than in men. This might allow more information to be exchanged between the two sides.

5 If so, perhaps it accords with the theory that in men the left hemisphere of the brain is more specialized for verbal abilities than it is in women. And men seem to use the right side of their brain when working on an abstract problem, while women use both sides.

6 How this might influence masculine and feminine modes of thinking science doesn't yet know. We do know, though, that brain development in the fetus is affected by hormones as well as genetics. And most of us grow up to think at least a little like the opposite sex.

7 The following quiz, based on surveys of some 2,000 people, could help you find out how male or female *your* brain is:

1. *You hear an indistinct meow. Without looking around, how well can you place the cat?*

   (a) If you think about it, you can point to it.
   (b) You can point straight to it.
   (c) You don't know if you can point to it.

2. *How good are you at remembering a song you've just heard?*

   (a) You find it easy, and you can sing part of it in tune.
   (b) You can do it only if it's simple and rhythmical.
   (c) You find it difficult.

3. *A person you've met a few times telephones you. How easy is it for you to recognize that voice in the few seconds before the person identifies himself?*

   (a) You find it quite easy.
   (b) You recognize the voice at least half the time.
   (c) You recognize the voice less than half the time.

4. *You're with a group of married friends. Two of them are having an affair. Would you detect this?*

   (a) Nearly always.
   (b) Half the time.
   (c) Seldom.

5. *You're introduced to five strangers at a large social gathering. If their names are mentioned the following day, how easy is it for you to picture their faces?*

   (a) You remember most of them.
   (b) You remember a few of them.
   (c) You seldom remember any of them.

6. *In your early school days, how easy was spelling and the writing of essays?*

   (a) Both were quite easy.
   (b) One was easy.
   (c) Neither was easy.

7. *You spot a parking place, but you must reverse into it—and it's going to be a fairly tight squeeze:*

   (a) You look for another space.
   (b) You back into it–carefully.
   (c) You reverse into it without much thought.

8. *You've spent three days in an unfamiliar village and someone asks you which way is north:*

   (a) You're unlikely to know.
   (b) You're not sure, but given a moment you can work it out.
   (c) You point north.

9. *You're in a dentist's waiting room. How close can you sit to people of the same sex as yourself without feeling uncomfortable?*

   (a) Less than six inches.
   (b) Six inches to two feet.
   (c) Over two feet.

10. *You're visiting your new neighbor, and the two of you are talking. There's a tap dripping in the background. Otherwise the room is quiet:*

    (a) You notice the dripping sound immediately and try to ignore it.
    (b) If you notice it, you probably mention it.
    (c) It doesn't bother you at all.

Scoring the Test

Males:
For each (a) answer, give 10 points.
For each (b) answer, give 5 points.
For each (c) answer, give -5 points.

Females:
For each (a) answer, give 15 points.
For each (b) answer, give 5 points.
For each (c) answer, give -5 points.

Unanswered questions count 5 points.

Most males will score between zero and 60. Most females will score between 50 and 100. The overlap—scores between 50 and 60—indicates a thought compatibility between the sexes.

Male scores below zero and female scores above 100 point to a brain very differently "wired" from that of the opposite sex. Male scores above 60 *may* show a bias to female mental attributes. Females who score below 50 *may* show a brain bias to the male thought processes.

EXPANDING VOCABULARY

Answer the following questions.

1. Which word in paragraph 1 means *fascinating?*

   _____

2. Which word in paragraph 1 means *small and unimportant?*

   _____

3. Which word in paragraph 2 means *do better than?*

   _____

4. Which word in paragraph 2 is an antonym for *concrete?*

   _____

5. Which phrase in paragraph 3 signals a contrast?

   _____

6. Which word in paragraph 3 means *to be larger in number?*

   _____

(continued on the next page)

7. Which word in paragraph 3 is an example of a speech defect?

   _____

8. Which phrase in paragraph 5 means *agrees with*?

   _____

9. Which word in paragraph 6 means *the manner* or *way*?

   _____

TALK IT OVER

DISCUSSION
QUESTIONS

1. How accurate do you think the quiz is in determining how you think?

2. Do you think males and females are treated differently by their teachers in school?

3. According to a Gallup poll,[1] the ten most frequently named characteristics for men are, in order:

aggressive	courageous	ambitious
strong	confident	selfish
proud	independent	logical
disorganized		

   The ten most frequently named characteristics for women are:

emotional	patient	cautious
talkative	romantic	creative
sensitive	moody	thrifty
affectionate		

   Do you agree with the words on the lists? Which words would you change?

TYING IT ALL TOGETHER

WORD FORMS

A. Complete the chart by filling in the missing forms of the words. The verb forms have been given.

VERB	NOUN	ADJECTIVE	ADVERB
behave			
comfort			
coordinate			
encourage			
flex			
relate			
resent			
respect			
speculate			
theorize			

B. Complete the sentences with words from the chart.

1. Even though I disagree with you, I _____ your opinions.

2. Although black holes in the universe _____ exist, no one has ever seen one.

3. Kazuo is the _____ of all of the special programs.

4. A good coach gives his team a lot of _____.

5. Doctors believe there is a _____ between stress and head colds.

(continued on the next page)

6. We can visit you any time this weekend; our plans are pretty
   _____.

7. Since we can't predict the future, we can only _____
   about what will happen next.

8. Five people can fit _____ in our new car.

9. Julie felt great _____ toward her sister for stealing
   her boyfriend.

10. The children were punished for their bad _____ during
    math class.

POSTREADING

DISCUSSION
QUESTIONS

1. Besides gender, in what ways are people different from each other? How
   are people alike? In general, do you think people around the world are
   more alike or different? Does diversity weaken or strengthen humankind?

2. How do social and cultural factors in the educational system of your country affect the development of boys and girls?

3. American Army General Douglas MacArthur said, "I promise to keep on
   living as though I expect to live forever. Nobody grows old by merely living
   a number of years. People grow old only by deserting their ideals. Years
   may wrinkle the skin, but to give up interest wrinkles the soul." What is
   your reaction to the quote?

JUST FOR FUN

TRICKY
QUESTIONS

**Answer the following "trick" questions. Then check your answers on page
229 of the Answer Key.**

1. You see a truck that has become stuck beneath an underpass because it
   was an inch too tall to continue passing through. There is a filling sta-
   tion and garage a short distance down the road. The driver of the truck
   is starting to walk toward the garage to get help when suddenly a
   bright idea pops into your head. You tell the driver, and five minutes
   later he is through the underpass and on his way.
      What did you tell him to do?

2. You are playing a game of Ping-Pong in the backyard of a friend's
   house. When you miss the ball, it bounces across the lawn and rolls
   into a small but deep hole. The hole goes down too far for you to reach
   the ball with your hand, and the hole bends so much to one side that

you can't get the ball by poking a stick into the hole. After a few minutes you think of an easy way to get the ball.

What did you think of?

3. Archibald Flapdoodle walked outside through pouring rain for twenty minutes without getting a single hair on his head wet. He didn't wear a hat, carry an umbrella, or hold anything over his head. His clothes got soaked.

How could this happen?

4. It takes twelve one-cent stamps to make a dozen. How many four-cent stamps does it take to make a dozen?

5. A Chicago lawyer and his wife went to Switzerland for a vacation. While they were skiing in the Alps, the wife skidded over a precipice and was killed. Back in Chicago an airline clerk read about the accident and immediately phoned the police. The lawyer was arrested and tried for murder.

The clerk did not know the lawyer or his wife. Nothing he'd heard or seen made him suspect foul play until he read about the accident in the paper.

Why did he call the police?

6. Bascom turned off the light in his bedroom and was able to get to bed before the room was dark. His bed is 15 feet from the wall switch.

How did Bascom do it?

7. How can you throw a ball so it goes a short distance, comes to a dead stop, reverses its motion, then goes the opposite way? You are not allowed to bounce it off anything, hit it with anything, or tie anything to it.

8. Why do barbers in Los Angeles prefer cutting the hair of ten fat men to cutting the hair of one skinny man?

READER'S JOURNAL

Choose a topic that relates to the readings in this unit and write for about ten to twenty minutes. Consider writing about one of the quotes in this unit or answering one of the discussion questions.

READER'S JOURNAL

Date: _____

THE AGE OF INFORMATION

Selections

Technology is changing our lives in ways that are hard to fathom. Nothing can stop the information revolution now that it has started. The way we work, study, communicate, and even entertain ourselves will never be the same again. The readings in this unit will require you to explore your own attitudes toward technology in today's changing world.

POINTS TO
PONDER

DISCUSSION
QUESTIONS

Think about and then discuss the following questions.

1. What technology-related words can you think of? Make a list of them and discuss their meanings with your classmates.

   _____   _____   _____

   _____   _____   _____

2. Do you own a computer? For what purposes do you use it? word processing? spreadsheets? games? electronic mail? software development? Internet?

3. Write down at least three ways that technology affects your daily life.

   _____

   _____

   _____

4. In general, do you think technology is making our lives easier or more complicated? In what ways? Explain your answer.

5. What makes this cartoon funny?

©1994, Washington Post Writers Group. Reprinted with permission.

As you read the articles in this unit, you may find it useful to refer to the dictionary of computer terms below to help you understand the specialized computer terms you will encounter. Read through these definitions once before you continue with the unit.

Dictionary of Computer Terms

1 **boot** *(verb)* to start a computer

2 **bug** *(noun)* a defect in a computer program

3 **computer virus** *(noun)* a program that damages files and can spread from one computer to another in a program

4 **cybernaut** *(noun)* someone who uses cyberspace

5 **cyberspace** *(noun)* refers to the whole range of information resources available through a computer network

6 **e-mail** *(noun)* electronically transmitted messages sent from one person to one or more others by computer

7 **emoticons** *(noun)* symbols used in e-mail messages to convey feelings

8 **file** *(noun)* a collection of related data

9 **hacker** *(noun)* used to describe someone who is capable of solving difficult computer problems, but not in a sophisticated manner

10 **hardware** *(noun)* the physical equipment of a computer

11 **Internet** *(noun)* a large public network connecting many smaller networks all over the world

12 **keyboard** *(noun)* a group of keys on a computer terminal or typewriter; *(verb)* to type as on a computer terminal or typewriter

13 **keystroke** *(noun)* pressing of a key as on a computer terminal or typewriter

14 **log on** *(verb)* to enter into a computer system

15 **modem** *(noun)* a device that allows a computer to transmit information over a phone line

16 **Net** *(noun)* slang; abbreviation for Internet

17 **network** *(noun)* an interconnected group or system

18 **online** *(adjective)* connected to a computer, as in *an online service*; *(adverb)* as in *to communicate online*

19 **software** *(noun)* a program that a computer uses to operate

The use of electronic mail (commonly known as e-mail) has exploded over the course of the last few years. E-mail has become an important part of the communications network for many offices and universities. But not everyone is happy about the increase in electronic forms of communication. In **TALK *to me*,** Nathan Cobb, a reporter for the *Boston Globe*, gives his opinion about e-mail.

1. Have you ever used e-mail? Do you have an e-mail address? If so, how often do you check your e-mail messages? What do you use e-mail for?

2. In general, do you feel more comfortable saying something to someone on the telephone, face to face, or via e-mail?

TALK *to me*

BY   NATHAN   COBB

1   Can the rumor be true? Can the people who run the place where I work really be considering setting a limit on the use of electronic mail? Or, can they actually be thinking of putting a stop to it? If so, I volunteer to pull the plug.

2   Am I wrong, or is e-mail an overrated phenomenon? The claims about sending correspondence from computer to computer are grandiose. You would think that e-mail—which is seldom used for conveying an idea more complex than "Let's have lunch"—is the greatest thing since Gutenberg invented the printing press. That's *Johann* Gutenberg, incidentally. Not guten@mainz.com.

3   Imagine for a moment that it was e-mail and not the telephone that was invented in 1876. Now imagine that it was the telephone and not e-mail that was developed a century later. Wouldn't we all be junking our keyboards while touting the phone as the hot new communications medium of the moment? No more typing, boss! We can actually hear each other!

4   But no. Many of us are thrilled to let our fingers do the talking. The absurdity of this is most evident in offices where private e-mail systems allow people who sit a few meters from one another to communicate via computer. Which they gladly do. (Or in the office where I work, "Message me.") What ever happened to "Talk to me"?

5   People who adore e-mail—and there is no shortage of them—love to say that it is convenient. They point out that the recipient doesn't even have to be at the receiving end, that the message can simply be left for

him or her. Well, I leave handwritten notes for my wife on the kitchen table all the time, and nobody seems to think it's a communications revolution. E-mail fans also like to point out that their favorite medium is fast-fast-fast. But since when is typing faster than speaking? Only when you can type faster than 200 or so words per minute, that's when.

6   OK: Let's concede that e-mail is useful if you want to drop a line to, say, 342 people at one time. And let's concede that it's a relatively cheap way for someone in Boston to leave a message for someone in Kanchipuram, India, assuming that both parties are armed with computers, modems, and the required level of Internet literacy. But taking a trip through cyberspace to communicate with someone at the next desk, down the hall, or even in a branch office? Please.

7   You don't have to use e-mail for long to realize its down side. It eliminates face-to-face conversation and everything that goes with it. Gone are tone of voice, nuance, and individuality. Gone are audio and visual clues to personality. Gone is any sense of self, replaced by text that looks the same no matter who is typing at the other end.

8   Admittedly, none of this signals the end of civilization as we know it. A few e-mail messages a day seems pretty harmless. The problem comes when these messages isolate the people at their desks, discouraging them from looking one another in the eye. When we are cut off from co-workers, our sense of community and common purpose withers.

9   In the place where I work, we no longer chat or gossip very much. The messages that we send are so lifeless that cybernauts have invented a bunch of symbols called "emoticons" to convey feelings. Meanwhile, people are wondering why morale is low. What this office needs—what this country needs—is more water coolers. And fewer keystrokes.

10 Sadly, it is customary for many journalists these days to publish their e-mail addresses at the end of their stories or columns. This supposedly makes them more "accessible." What it really does, of course, is make them reachable to the relatively small number of people who own computers and modems compared to folks who own telephones. It's elitist. So please, don't try me at cobb@nws.globe.com. I'll be at 929-2961 instead.

Which of the following statements do you think the author would agree with? Put a check mark next to those statements.

_____ 1. E-mail is an overrated phenomenon.

_____ 2. E-mail is often used to send important and complex messages.

_____ 3. E-mail is as important as the invention of the printing press.

_____ 4. Since the telephone was invented first, it is much more popular than e-mail.

_____ 5. If e-mail had been invented before the telephone, it would be the most popular communications medium.

_____ 6. If the telephone were a new invention, people would claim that it was much better than e-mail.

_____ 7. There are many people who love e-mail because they think it is convenient.

_____ 8. E-mail is a very convenient medium of communication.

_____ 9. It is ridiculous for people in the same office to use e-mail to communicate with each other.

_____ 10. E-mail is depersonalizing and isolating.

_____ 11. People who work in offices should spend less time talking and more time working.

_____ 12. E-mail is an elitist form of communication.

Now go back and decide which of the statements you agree with. Put your initials next to those statements. Discuss your opinions with your classmates.

Choose the word or phrase from the list that is closest in meaning to the highlighted word in each sentence. Write the answer on the line provided.

throwing out	admit	govern	dries up
foolishness	available	delighted	
thing	spirit	impressive	

1. _Can the people who **run** the place where I work really be considering setting a limit on the use of electronic mail?_

2. *Am I wrong, or is e-mail an overrated **event**?*

_____

3. *The claims about sending correspondence from computer to computer are **excessive.**_

_____

4. *Wouldn't we all be **junking** our keyboards while touting the phone as the hot new communications medium of the moment?*

_____

5. *The **absurdity** of this is most evident in offices where private e-mail systems allow people who sit a few meters from one another to communicate via computer.*

_____

6. *Many of us are **thrilled** to let our fingers do the talking.*

_____

7. *Let's **concede** that e-mail is useful if you want to drop a line to, say, 342 people at one time.*

_____

8. *When we are cut off from co-workers, our sense of community and common purpose **withers.**_

_____

9. *Meanwhile, people are wondering why **morale** is low.*

_____

10. *This supposedly makes them more **accessible.**_

_____

FYi

Only one message in four that goes over telephone lines is an actual phone conversation.

FIGURE IT OUT

IDIOMS

Match the idioms on the left with their meanings on the right. Use the context from the paragraphs to help you figure out the meanings.

IDIOMS	MEANINGS
_____ 1. pull the plug (¶1)	a. direct, personal
_____ 2. point out (¶5)	b. meet with a steady look
_____ 3. drop a line (¶6)	c. stop something
_____ 4. armed with (¶6)	d. possess
_____ 5. down side (¶7)	e. write a note
_____ 6. face-to-face (¶7)	f. emphasize
_____ 7. look (someone) in the eye (¶8)	g. separate
_____ 8. cut off (¶8)	h. disadvantages

Now use each idiom in a sentence of your own.

1. _____

2. _____

3. _____

4. _____

5. _____

6. _____

7. _____

8. _____

TALK IT OVER

DISCUSSION
QUESTIONS

1. In what ways does the author think that e-mail makes people feel isolated? Do you agree or disagree with his opinion?

2. The author mentions several negative aspects of e-mail. What positive aspects can you think of?

3. Would you rather meet with old friends online or in person? What about new friends? Do you think you would feel more comfortable communicating with someone you don't know online or face to face?

ACROSS TIME

Read the following selection as quickly as possible and decide which title is the most appropriate. Write the title on the line.

1. Why Is It So Difficult to Take a Break from Work?

2. Faxing Grandpa

3. The Technology Boom Makes Life Easier

4. Data-Gathering in the Nineties

The technology boom adds a peculiar twist to stress in the '90s. Certainly, our ancestors worked hard with less sophisticated tools. Grandma stoically stocked wood for the stove every morning and scrubbed laundry on a washboard. Grandpa clocked in long, arduous hours on the railroad, or in the mines. But when he came home, there were no faxes waiting for him to answer, no cellular phones or e-mail to interrupt his after supper smoke. Home was home, not a pit stop for data-gathering before heading back to the office. Today, there is no down time, no escape—from work or from other people. We have cellular phones in our cars and beepers in our pockets, and we carry them to Disneyland, to the beach, to the bathroom. It means, says Boston University Medical Center's Dr. Mark Moskowitz, that "a lot of people are working 24 hours per day, seven days a week, even when they're not technically at work."[1]

Although many women have entered traditionally male fields such as law and medicine, a significantly fewer number have chosen to enter the computer industry. This fact may help to explain why the world of computers is still dominated by men. In **Gender Gap in Cyberspace,** professor and author Deborah Tannen examines the differing attitudes that men and women have toward their computers and emerging technologies.

BEFORE YOU READ

PREREADING DISCUSSION

The following quotes are taken from a recent article entitled "Men, Women and Computers."[2] Read the quotes and discuss them with your classmates. Do you think these ideas are accurate? Do they reflect real differences in attitude between the sexes?

1. "Men tend to be seduced by the technology. They get into the faster-race-car syndrome, bragging about the speed of their microprocessors."

   "Women are much more practical, much more interested in the machine's utility. 'I don't really care about its innards. I just want to do the job.'"

2. "Men typically imagine devices that could help them conquer the universe. Men think of machines as an extension of their physical power."

   "Women want machines that meet people's needs, the perfect mother. And one that can be turned on and off at the flick of a switch."

3. "The vast majority of videogame designers are men: they make games they want to play. Why do you think it's called Game Boy?"

   "Girls tend to prefer nonlinear games, where there's more than one way to win. Some even dislike having characters die on screen."

Gender Gap in Cyberspace

MEN WANT TO FORCE COMPUTERS TO SUBMIT.
WOMEN JUST WANT COMPUTERS TO WORK.

BY DEBORAH TANNEN

1   *I* was a computer pioneer, but I'm still something of a novice. That paradox is telling.

2   I was the second person on my block to get a computer. The first was my colleague Ralph. It was 1980. Ralph got a Radio Shack TRS-80; I got a used Apple II+. He helped me get started and went on to become a maven, reading computer magazines, hungering for the new technology he read about, and buying and mastering it as quickly as he could afford. I hung on to old equipment far too long because I dislike giving up what I'm used to, fear making the wrong decision about what to buy and resent the time it takes to install and learn a new system.

3   My first Apple came with videogames; I gave them away. Playing games on the computer didn't interest me. If I had free time I'd spend it talking on the telephone to friends.

4   Ralph got hooked. His wife was often annoyed by the hours he spent at his computer and the money he spent upgrading it. My marriage had no such strains—until I discovered e-mail. Then I got hooked. E-mail draws me the same way the phone does: it's a souped-up conversation.

5   E-mail deepened my friendship with Ralph. Though his office was next to mine, we rarely had extended conversations because he is shy. Face to face he mumbled so, I could barely tell he was speaking. But when we both got e-mail, I started receiving long, self-revealing messages; we poured our hearts out to each other. A friend discovered that e-mail opened up that kind of communication with her father. He would never talk much on the phone (as her mother would), but they have become close since they both got on line.

6   Why, I wondered, would some men find it easier to open up on e-mail? It's a combination of the technology (which they enjoy) and the obliqueness of the written word, just as many men will reveal feelings in dribs and drabs while riding in the car or doing something, which they'd never talk about sitting face to face. It's too intense, too bearing-down on them, and once you start you have to keep going. With a computer in between, it's easier.

7   It was on e-mail, in fact, that I described to Ralph how boys in groups often struggle to get the upper hand whereas girls tend to maintain an appearance of cooperation. And he pointed out that this explained why boys are more likely to be captivated by computers than girls are. Boys are typically motivated by a social structure that says if you don't dominate you will be dominated. Computers, by their nature, balk: you type a perfectly appropriate command and it refuses to do what it should. Many boys and men are incited by this

defiance: "I'm going to whip this into line and teach it who's boss! I'll get it to do what I say!" (and if they work hard enough, they always can). Girls and women are more likely to respond, "This thing won't cooperate. Get it away from me!"

8   Although no one wants to think of herself as "typical," my relationship to my computer is fairly typical for a woman. Most women (with plenty of exceptions) aren't excited by tinkering with the technology, grappling with the challenge of eliminating bugs or getting the biggest and best computer. These dynamics appeal to many men's interest in making sure they're on the top side of the inevitable who's-up-who's-down struggle that life is for them. E-mail appeals to my view of life as a contest for connections to others. When I see that I have 15 messages I feel loved.

9   I once posted a technical question on a computer network for linguists and was flooded with long dispositions, some pages long. I was staggered by the generosity and the expertise, but wondered where these guys found the time—and why all the answers I got were from men.

10   Like coed classrooms and meetings, discussions on e-mail networks tend to be dominated by male voices, unless they're specifically women-only, like single-sex schools. On line, women don't have to worry about getting the floor (you just send a message when you feel like it), but, according to linguists Susan Herring and Laurel Sutton, who have studied this, they have the usual problems of having their messages ignored or attacked. The anonymity of public networks frees a small number of men to send long, vituperative, sarcastic messages that many other men either can tolerate or actually enjoy, but turn most women off. The anonymity of networks leads to another sad part of the e-mail story: there are men who deluge women with questions about their appearance.

11   **Taking time** Most women want one thing from a computer—to work. This is significant counterevidence to the claim that men want to focus on information while women are interested in rapport. That claim I found was often true in casual conversation, in which there is no particular informa-tion to be conveyed. But with computers, it is often women who are more focused on information, because they don't respond to the challenge of getting equipment to submit.

12   Once I had learned the basics, my interest in computers waned. I use it to write books (though I never mastered having it do bibliographies or tables of contents) and write checks (but not balance my checkbook). Much as I'd like to use it to do more, I begrudge the time it would take to learn.

13   Ralph's computer expertise costs him a lot of time. Chivalry requires that he rescue novices in need, and he is called upon by damsel novices far more often than knaves. More men would rather study the instruction booklet than ask directions, as it were, from another person. "When I do help men," Ralph wrote (on e-mail, of course), "they want to be more involved. I once installed a hard drive for a guy, and he wanted to be there with me, wielding the screwdriver and giving his own advice where he could." Women, he finds, usually are not interested in what he's doing; they just want him to get the computer to the point where they can do what they want.

14   Which pretty much explains how I managed to be a pioneer without becoming an expert.

DEBORAH TANNEN *is a university professor at Georgetown University and author of the* best seller You Just Don't Understand: Women and Men in Conversation.

BUILDING READING SKILLS

EXAMINING CONTRASTS

Deborah Tannen develops her article by contrasting her own approach to computers with that of her colleague Ralph. Decide whether Deborah or Ralph would be more likely to do each of the following. Put a check mark in the appropriate column.

Who would be more likely to...

	Deborah	Ralph	Both
1. spend hours talking with a friend on the phone?			
2. go to a computer store to check out the most recent models?			
3. spend the afternoon helping neighbors set up their new computer?			
4. give away computer games?			
5. balance a checkbook on the computer?			
6. send an e-mail message?			
7. get frustrated and give up easily when the computer isn't working properly?			
8. study the instruction booklet if the computer is having a problem?			
9. keep a computer for many years?			
10. buy the latest computer equipment?			

A. Circle the letter of the word or phrase that is closest in meaning to the highlighted idiom in each sentence.

1. *I **hung on to** old equipment far too long because I dislike giving up what I'm used to . . .*

   a. threw out
   b. kept
   c. bought

2. *Ralph **got hooked**. His wife was often annoyed by the hours he spent at his computer and the money he spent upgrading it.*

   a. became addicted
   b. got bored
   c. was upset

3. *But when we both got on e-mail, I started receiving long, self-revealing messages. We **poured our hearts out** to each other.*

   a. talked about everything
   b. served coffee
   c. kept secrets

4. *Some men find it easier **to open up** on e-mail.*

   a. start the program
   b. go faster
   c. reveal feelings

5. *Many men will reveal feelings **in dribs and drabs** while riding in the car or doing something, which they'd never talk about sitting face to face.*

   a. in large pieces
   b. in small bits
   c. with enthusiasm

6. *Boys in groups often struggle **to get the upper hand** whereas girls tend to maintain an appearance of cooperation.*

   a. use their hands
   b. be a good sport
   c. get control

7. *I'm going **to whip this into line** and teach it who's boss!*

   a. get this to perform well
   b. draw lines on it
   c. hit it with a whip

Men earning computer science degrees outnumber women three to one and the gap is growing, according to the National Science Foundation.[3]

8. *I once posted a technical question on a computer network for linguists and* ***was flooded with*** *long [messages], some pages long.*

   a. lost several
   b. sent many
   c. received many

9. *On line, women don't have to worry about* ***getting the floor,*** *you just send a message when you feel like it . . .*

   a. commanding attention
   b. acting feminine
   c. being too busy

B. Answer the following questions.

1. If you want to point out that you disagree with what everyone at a meeting is saying, should you try *to get the floor,* or should you wait quietly until someone asks for your opinion?

   _____

   _____

   _____

The ratio of men to women on the World Wide Web is 85:15. The ratio of men to women using online services is 65:35.

2. If you are afraid to *look someone in the eye,* would you want to have a *face-to-face* conversation with him or send him an e-mail message?

   _____

   _____

   _____

3. If you don't want *to open up* to someone, would you *pour your heart out* to her or would you say little?

   _____

   _____

   _____

(continued on the next page)

4. If you're *hooked on* antique cars, would you *hang on* to your grandfather's 1915 Model T or give it away?

_____

_____

_____

5. If you want *to drop someone a line*, would you call him on the phone or send him an e-mail message?

_____

_____

_____

BUILDING WRITING SKILLS

SUMMARIZING

Write a short summary of Deborah Tannen's opinions about gender differences in cyberspace.

_____

_____

_____

_____

_____

_____

TALK IT OVER

DISCUSSION QUESTIONS

1. According to the author, how do men and women behave differently in groups? How is this difference reflected in their respective interest in computers?

2. Why does the author think some men find it easy to open up on e-mail?

3. According to the author, the anonymity of public networks has several negative effects on the behavior of some e-mail users. Discuss these effects.

4. Do you agree with the author's observations? How much validity do you think they have?

It is not surprising that the growth in computer use has been accompanied by a growth in computer crimes. The last few years have brought dramatic changes in the range and nature of computer-related crimes. Unfortunately, neither laws nor law enforcement officers are equipped to deal with the rich variety of criminal activity that now proliferates. This article, **Cracking Down on Computer Crime,** provides a look at some types of computer crime and some ways that police are trying to deal with them.

BEFORE YOU READ

PREREADING QUESTIONS

1. Make a list of the types of computer crime that you are familiar with.

   _____

   _____

   _____

   _____

2. Do you consider it a crime to borrow a computer game or program from a friend and make a copy of it for yourself? Why or why not?

BUILDING READING SKILLS

SKIMMING

Skimming is a fast and easy method of finding out what important ideas will be discussed in a passage. Read the article one time quickly and list the types of computer crimes the author mentions. Then compare this list to the one you made in the prereading exercise.

   _____

   _____

   _____

   _____

   _____

Now read the article again more carefully and do the exercises that follow it.

Cracking Down on Computer Crime

By Erik Markus

1   San Diego police detective Dennis Sadler got a tip. A homeowner had discovered a suspicious-looking list of numbers in a room he was renting to a teen-ager.

2   That list led to the teen-ager's arrest. The numbers on it had come from credit cards and could be used in place of cash to buy things illegally.

3   More importantly, the list helped Detective Sadler break up a nation-wide network of "hackers." These young people were using their home computers to break the law.

4   The hackers, who lived in Ohio, New York, California and other states, had hooked their computers to tele-phone lines. Then, over the phone, they had electronically broken into the computers of national credit card agencies. The hackers created phony credit card accounts and used them to make millions of dollars' worth of purchases—without paying.

5   "One kid bragged about using the same credit card number for eight months," Detective Sadler says.

6   Such computer crime is on the rise. It is so new and complicated that most police departments don't know how to handle it. For that reason, the Federal Bureau of Investigation (F.B.I.) and the Secret Service have teamed up to help.

7   The growing wave of high-tech crime includes:

8   *Credit Card Criminals.* The worst of computer crime appears to be credit card fraud, as already described. Officials from the Secret Service say it causes worldwide losses of up to $3.5 billion each year.

9   Police recently nabbed a 19-year-old southern California man who checked into a $400-a-night hotel suite in Palm Springs, Calif.

10   He was planning to pay the bill by re-encoding the magnetic strip on his own credit card to another person's credit card number.

11   How? "[Criminals] can buy a re-encoder," says Jim Miller. He's the assistant special agent in charge of the Los Angeles office of the Secret Service. "[Then they] erase the old

Computer
criminals
cause billions
of dollars'
worth of
losses and
damages.

information and put in the new information. That's a scary situation."

12 Two of the nation's largest credit card companies are working on a plan that would prevent such re-encoding.

13 *Phone Phreaks.* Another area of growing concern is theft of long-distance telephone service. Sprint, a long-distance phone company, reports that this fraud approaches $1 billion annually.

14 Typically, these "phone phreaks" call a long-distance company on a toll-free number. Using a computer, they figure out the codes necessary to gain access to an outgoing line. Then they use the line to make calls anywhere in the world.

15 *Legion of Doom.* In 1990, the Secret Service launched "Operation Sundevil." Agents raided suspected computer bandits in 14 states. The agents hauled away 42 computers and 23,000 diskettes.

16 The target of the 150 gun-packing agents was a nationwide network of hackers called the "Legion of Doom." Members of this group were suspected of trading long-distance phone cards and stolen credit card numbers.

17 "Almost all the kids involved were below age 18," reports Miller.

18 *Making Computers Sick.* Another type of computer crime is sabotage.

The criminal uses his or her skills to damage computer files or programs. Angry employees have done this to the big computers in the offices where they work.

19 Particularly harmful are criminals who install a "virus" into a computer system. Viruses are programs that can damage files and bring businesses to a halt. And they can spread from computer to computer much as a biological virus spreads from person to person.

20 In 1988, a graduate student named Robert Morris created a virus that crippled a nationwide network of government and university computers. A judge sentenced him to three years' probation, a $10,000 fine and 400 hours of community service.

21 No one has caught the creator of Michelangelo. That 1992 virus caused millions of dollars' worth of damage to computers worldwide.

22 Perhaps the worst virus is called the Pakistani Brain. It was designed to be especially difficult to find. Infected computer disks have spread the virus around the world since 1986.

23 But antivirus companies have sprung to the rescue. They make software which can find and destroy most virus programs.

24 *Spies.* Other criminals use computers to spy. They steal secrets from one company or government and sell them to another. Spies have used phones, modems, computers and simple software to get information illegally.

25 Cliff Stoll, who was in charge of computers for a Berkeley, Calif., physics lab, helped break up an espionage ring in 1988. After months of tracking a hacker who kept breaking into his research computers, he got the F.B.I. and the Central Intelligence Agency to help him.

26 The spy was traced to Germany. He had broken into more than 400 U.S. military and research computers. He was selling the information to the Soviet secret police, or K.G.B.

27 Stoll's story has been told in a best-selling book, "The Cuckoo's Egg."

28 *Software Piracy.* Yet another type of computer crime is to copy, or "pirate," computer games and software. People who get a pirated copy don't pay for a new one. Software manufacturers lose $1 billion a year this way.

> Law enforcers are quick to encourage a healthy interest in computers.

COMPUTERS SHOULD HELP US, NOT HURT US

29 Law enforcers want to arrest those hackers who break the law. But they are quick to encourage a healthy interest in computers.

30 Computers help us store knowledge and exchange ideas. They have become a powerful tool at both school and work. The challenge is to keep criminals from using computers to steal, or to hurt people in other ways.

31 To meet that challenge, law enforcement agencies need experts who can help them crack down on computer crime.

32 "We could use more people in police work with computer skills," says Detective Sadler.

33 Clint Howard of the Secret Service agrees. "We have a [group] of people carved out of the Secret Service who are intensely trained in computer crime areas," Howard says. "We call them our computer crime team."

34 Their full-time job: to crack down on computer crime.

HACKING IS ILLEGAL

"Anyone who breaks into a computer system is breaking the law."

So says San Diego Detective Dennis Sadler. These hackers, he explains, have broken into credit card systems, phone banks, major computer networks, automatic teller machines and other computer systems. "Even if it's done for fun, they are breaking state and/or Federal laws," he says.

And, he adds, that includes illegally copying computer games.

Many hackers are kids. Sadler cites three reasons why youths break into computer systems.

First, it's for the challenge. Sadler says most hackers remain at the challenge level.

"Hacking takes a lot of time," he explains. "Most kids have better things to do."

But some teen-age thrill seekers, after breaking into a system, step down to the next level of crime. That involves retrieving private information, such as credit card numbers.

Third, a small group of hackers reach the lowest level. These hackers actually use the information they retrieve to steal.

"These are the hardcore hackers," Sadler says. "These are the kids who'll wind up in prison when they're caught."

BUILDING READING SKILLS

RECOGNIZING MAIN IDEAS

Which of the following topics are discussed in the article? Put a check mark next to those topics.

_____ 1. the kinds of high-tech crimes that are on the rise

_____ 2. an explanation of computer viruses

_____ 3. the benefits of computers in education and business

_____ 4. the reasons young people break into computer systems

_____ 5. how the computer crime team is trained

_____ 6. the problems that computer crime can cause

HOW WELL DID YOU READ?

Read the following statements. If a statement is true, write _T_ on the line. If it is false, write _F_.

_____ 1. The most serious computer crime is credit card fraud.

_____ 2. There is less computer crime now than there was in the past.

_____ 3. Software companies lose a lot of money each year because of pirated computer games and software.

_____ 4. The FBI and the Secret Service have made a joint effort to stop computer crime.

_____ 5. Some criminals have used computers to spy on governments and businesses.

_____ 6. Computer hackers who break into phone banks just for fun are not committing a real crime.

_____ 7. The creator of the virus Michelangelo was sentenced to three years' probation and given a $10,000 fine.

1. How are computer viruses like biological viruses? How can computer viruses hurt businesses and other institutions?

2. Why are police departments having a hard time dealing with computer crime? What steps do you think they can take to help prevent computer crime?

3. What are "phone phreaks"? How do they commit their crimes?

4. How do credit card criminals commit their crimes? What are credit card companies doing to prevent this kind of crime?

5. Jim Thomas, a criminology professor at Northern Illinois University says, "The new computer crimes aren't simply the esoteric type they were five years ago. They are 'computer crimes' only in the sense that a bank robbery with a getaway car is an 'automobile crime.'"[4] Discuss what Thomas means by this statement.

TYING IT ALL TOGETHER

WORD FORMS

A. Complete the chart by filling in the missing forms of the words. The noun forms have been given.

VERB	NOUN	ADJECTIVE	ADVERB
	cooperation		
	correspondence correspondent		
	expansion expanse		
	generosity		
	imagination		
	persistence		
	reliance reliability		
	revelation		
	submission		
	suspicion suspect		

B. Correct the sentences that have errors in word forms.

1. The company's plans for <u>expand</u> will be very costly.

2. It is hard to <u>imagination</u> what the world will be like in 100 years.

(continued on the next page)

3. Arthur's <u>submissive</u> to his parents wishes is predictable.

4. My car is five years old, but it is still very <u>reliably</u>.

5. Brigitte and Pat <u>corresponded</u> with each other for many years.

6. It was very <u>generosity</u> of you to lend me your golf clubs yesterday.

7. He was arrested on the <u>suspect</u> of robbery.

8. Fran thanked her children for being so <u>cooperation</u> during the long car ride.

9. Sharon showed such <u>persist</u> that the company finally gave her a job.

10. Bill wrote a very <u>revealing</u> short story about his childhood.

POSTREADING

DISCUSSION QUESTIONS

1. Is technology making our lives simpler or more complex? In what ways?

2. Do you think technology enhances or dampens creativity? How? Defend your answer.

3. Discuss the consequences of technology in terms of each of the following: safety, health, business, school, entertainment, environment, and the arts.

4. Many people feel that technological advances such as CD-ROM and the Internet will make libraries obsolete. Others feel that computers will never replace books and libraries. Which opinion do you agree with? Why?

5. Is it possible to police cyberspace? What attempts do you think should be made to protect the rights of individuals and businesses from such things as pornography and computer crime?

JUST FOR FUN

EMOTICONS

Communicating in cyberspace can be fascinating, but without physical clues such as intonation and body language, it is often difficult to get your message across. For this reason, a whole set of symbols called **emoticons** has developed. Everything from a wink to sticking out your tongue can be conveyed with a few keystrokes.

With your classmates, see if you can match the e-mail emoticons on the left with their correct meanings on the right. Write the meaning on the line next to the emoticon. Hint: Try turning the page sideways to view some of the symbols as faces. Then check your answers on page 229 of the Answer Key.

EMOTICONS		MEANINGS
1. :)	_____	a. mad
2. :O	_____	b. happy
3. >:<	_____	c. sad
4. :D	_____	d. laughing
5. :-<	_____	e. really happy
6. :-/	_____	f. surprised
7. :-e	_____	g. disappointed
8. :(	_____	h. hugs
9. :,(	_____	i. kisses
10. :-o	_____	j. crying
11. :->	_____	k. screaming
12. :	_____	l. skeptical
13. :*	_____	m. really sad
14. []	_____	n. tired

READER'S JOURNAL

Choose a topic that relates to the readings in this unit and write for about ten to twenty minutes. Consider writing about one of the quotes in this unit or answering one of the discussion questions.

READER'S JOURNAL

Date: _____

_____

_____

_____

_____

_____

_____

_____

_____

_____

_____

_____

_____

_____

_____

_____

_____

_____

_____

_____

_____

_____

THE BEAUTY OF SCIENCE

FYi

Unit·7

Selections

"We go about our daily lives understanding almost nothing of the world. We give little thought to the machinery that generates the sunlight that makes life possible, to the gravity that glues us to an Earth that would otherwise send us spinning off into space, or to the atoms of which we are made and on whose stability we fundamentally depend. Except for children (who don't know enough not to ask the important questions), few of us spend much time wondering why nature is the way it is; where the cosmos comes from, or whether it was always here; if time will one day flow backward and effects precede causes; or whether there are ultimate limits to what humans can know."[1] Carl Sagan, Astronomer

POINTS TO PONDER

DISCUSSION
QUESTIONS

Think about and then discuss the following questions.

1. How much time do you spend wondering about the world you live in? What five questions does Carl Sagan ask? How would you answer each question?

2. In your opinion, are children more curious than adults? Do they ask better questions? Explain your point of view.

Reprinted courtesy of Howard Post.

Stephen William Hawking is a British theoretical physicist and probably the best-known scientist alive today. He has been called one of the most brilliant theoretical physicists since Albert Einstein. Hawking obtained his doctorate from the University of Cambridge, where he is the Lucasian Professor of Mathematics, a title once held by Isaac Newton. Much of his work deals with the concept of black holes. Hawking has made many important contributions to science while battling amyotrophic lateral sclerosis (ALS), an incurable disease of the nervous system. In **Hawking Gets Personal,** you will read about his latest book.

1. Do you like to look at the sky at night? What do you think about when you gaze at the stars?

2. What do you know about black holes? What are they? Where do they come from?

Hawking Gets Personal

BY MICHAEL D. LEMONICK

The author of the best-selling A Brief History of Time tries a new formula: less cosmology, more about himself.

1 For the past hour, the attention of a group of wheelchair-bound teenagers in a Seattle auditorium has been completely focused on the man seated in front of them. Such self-control would be unusual for teens in any case; it's even more impressive considering that the speaker is a theoretical astrophysicist. Stephen Hawking has a few advantages, though. For one, the 51-year-old Cambridge University professor is probably the best-known scientist in the world. For another, Hawking is in a wheelchair too, the victim of a degenerative nerve disease that has left him as paralyzed as his youthful audience.

2 But what really has the kids' attention is that Hawking did a guest spot

171

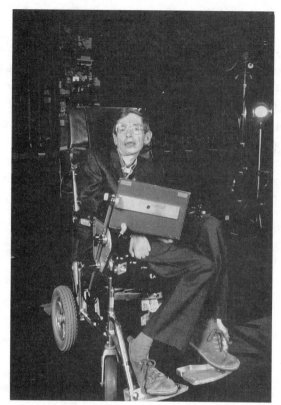

Hawking's body is paralyzed; his mind roams the cosmos.

last season on *Star Trek: The Next Generation,* playing a time-bending game of poker with his intellectual forebears, Albert Einstein and Sir Isaac Newton. The cameo appearance won him almost as much popular recognition as *A Brief History of Time,* the 1988 best seller that spent 53 weeks on the *New York Times* list, sold an astounding 5.5 million copies worldwide and spawned and award-winning movie. Not bad for a volume that was, despite its billing as an easy read, nearly impossible to get through.

3   Now Hawking's new book, *Black Holes and Baby Universes* (Bantam; $21.95), is en route to stores and getting nearly as big a buildup as the latest John Grisham thriller. Why, when his days are already overcrowded with

scientific meetings, lecture tours and the occasional sit-down with disabled kids, did he take the time to write a new book? "I had to pay for my nurses," Hawking says (or, rather, since he can't speak, his computer-driven voice synthesizer intones, in a voice something like Lawrence Welk's).

4   The answer is typical Hawking—droll, irreverent and totally honest. He needs nursing care around the clock, and even the distinguished Lucasian Professorship of Mathematics at Cambridge, a seat once held by Newton, doesn't pay enough to cover it. A victim of Lou Gehrig's disease (amyotrophic lateral sclerosis, or ALS). Hawking can move only some facial muscles and one finger on his left hand, which he uses to pick out words on a computer touch-screen attached to his motorized wheelchair. He can search through the computer's dictionary by selecting the first letter or two of a word or by choosing from a menu of frequently used phrases and sentences.

5   Though Hawking argues that the public bought his first book largely because of the ideas it contained, his readers were probably just as interested in the man himself. "No one can resist the idea of a crippled genius," Hawking says, with an edge of displeasure. He is not, as some have claimed, the second coming of Einstein, a characterization Hawking denounces as "rubbish . . . mere media hype." But his work on black holes, especially, would be of Nobel caliber—except that the prize committee insists that theoretical work has to be verified by experiment or observation before it is rewarded. None of Hawking's theories will likely be proved during his lifetime, a fact that

Hawking claims doesn't bother him. "It is better to go on and make new discoveries than to hope for a prize for work I did years ago." His current interest: trying to determine whether elementary particles that fall into black holes can form new, baby universes, forever cut off from ours.

6   Unlike *A Brief History,* the new book (a collection of essays, transcribed talks and new writings) contains plenty about Hawking himself. There are the requisite discussions of quantum physics and cosmology, of course. But those millions who bought yet couldn't penetrate *A Brief History* may be relieved to hear that there are also chapters on Hawking's early life, his marriage to fellow student Jane Wilde and his experiences as an ALS victim.

7   Readers will learn, for example, that his father was a doctor who did research on tropical diseases, and his mother a secretary. The family was considered somewhat eccentric—they drove around in an old London taxi because they couldn't afford a new car. Hawking didn't concentrate much on his studies in college, and gave up completely for a while when his ALS was diagnosed. But his marriage, and the need to support a family, got him to start working hard for the first time in his life. "To my surprise," he writes, "I found I liked it," and his career took off.

8   The new book also addresses, at least in passing, a controversy stirred by *A Brief History.* Many readers interpreted portions of that book as an attempt to disprove the existence of God. Not so, says Hawking. "You don't need to appeal to God to set the initial conditions for the universe, but that doesn't prove there is no God—only that he acts through the laws of physics." Other controversies are ignored. Three years ago, Hawking left his wife after more than two decades and moved in with Elaine Mason, one of his nurses. "I would rather not go into details of my private life," is all he will say.

9   The kids in the lecture hall have other things on their mind besides black holes and broken marriages. As Hawking finishes, they crowd around him, forming a semicircle of wheelchairs, and begin pelting him with questions on topics closer to home: "How do you make a legal signature if you can't write?" "How do you feel about the Americans with Disabilities Act?" "What are Klingons really like?" As they wait for Hawking to tap out his answers, they can't stop grinning. Here's a famous scientist, a bestselling author, a *Star Trek* star—and he's disabled, just like them.

● ●

HOW WELL DID YOU READ?   **Read the following statements. If a statement is true, write *T* on the line. If it is false, write *F*.**

_____ 1. Most people found Hawking's book *A Brief History of Time* easy to read.

_____ 2. Hawking is able to communicate through a computer-driven voice synthesizer.

(continued on the next page)

_____ 3. Hawking won a Nobel prize for his work on black holes.

_____ 4. Hawking claims to be the second Einstein.

_____ 5. Hawking's new book *Black Holes and Baby Universes* contains more personal information than his previous book.

_____ 6. *A Brief History of Time* is Hawking's attempt to disprove the existence of god.

BUILDING READING SKILLS

EXAMINING MEANING

Read each of the following sentences from the article carefully. Then, circle the letter of the sentence that is closest in meaning to the numbered ones.

1. *A Brief History of Time . . . sold an astounding 5.5 million copies . . . . Not bad for a volume that was, despite its billing as an easy read, nearly impossible to get through.*

   a. Since *A Brief History of Time* is interesting and easy to read, it sold millions of copies.
   b. It is too bad that *A Brief History of Time* is so difficult to read. Therefore, not many people bought it.
   c. Although *A Brief History of Time* is difficult to read, it was a surprisingly popular book.

When soil brought back from the surface of the moon was analyzed, it proved to be about 4,600 million years old.

2. *Though Hawking argues that the public bought his first book largely because of the ideas it contained, his readers were probably just as interested in the man himself.*

   a. Hawking believes that his first book was so popular because many readers were interested in finding out about his life.
   b. Hawking argues with his readers who disagree with his ideas and disapprove of his life.
   c. Contrary to what Hawking believes, many people who bought his first book were just as interested in finding out about his life as reading about his theories.

3. *But his work on black holes, especially, would be of Nobel caliber—except that the prize committee insists that theoretical work has to be verified by experiment or observation before it is rewarded.*

   a. Hawking's work on black holes has not received a Nobel prize because it has not been proven.
   b. The Noble prize committee plans to give Hawking an award for his work on black holes.
   c. Hawking's work on black holes is not important enough to be considered for a Nobel prize.

4. *None of Hawking's theories will likely be proved during his lifetime, a fact that Hawking claims doesn't bother him.*

   a. Hawking is probably upset that none of his theories will be proved during his lifetime.
   b. Hawking is working desperately to prove his theories before he dies.
   c. Hawking doesn't mind that he probably will not live long enough to see his theories proven.

5. *The new book also addresses, at least in passing, a controversy stirred by A Brief History.*

   a. The new book is more controversial than *A Brief History*.
   b. The new book deals superficially with a controversy that grew out of *A Brief History*.
   c. The new book ignores a controversy that *A Brief History* dealt with.

FIGURE IT OUT

IDIOMS

Look back through the article and underline each of the following idiomatic expressions. Then, using context from the paragraph and the sentences provided, write a definition for each one. Finally, write your own sentence that expresses the meaning of the idiom.

1. around the clock (¶4)

   When I have a deadline, I work *around the clock* until my work is finished.

   definition: _____

   sentence: _____

   _____

2. pick out (¶4)

   My friend likes to *pick out* the perfect pair of shoes for every outfit.

   definition: _____

   sentence: _____

   _____

In 1983, a tiny fleck of paint hit the windshield of the spacecraft *Challenger* as it re-entered the earth's atmosphere, making so many holes in it that the entire windshield had to be replaced.

3. cut off (¶5)

   Without a telephone, I would feel *cut off* from my friends and family who live far away.

   definition: _____

   sentence: _____

   _____

(continued on the next page)

4. give up (¶7)

I'm planning to *give up* this job when school starts.

definition: _____

sentence: _____

_____

5. take off (¶7)

After she got the star role in a hit movie, her acting career seemed to *take off* overnight.

definition: _____

sentence: _____

_____

6. go into (¶8)

Let's talk about what happened at the meeting later. I don't want to *go into* it right now.

definition: _____

sentence: _____

_____

7. on one's mind (¶9)

I'm glad you want to discuss this problem because it's been *on my mind* for days.

definition: _____

sentence: _____

_____

READ AND REACT

Hawking said, "Although equations are a concise and accurate way of describing mathematical ideas, they frighten most people. When I wrote a popular book recently [referring to *A Brief History of Time*], I was advised that each equation I included would halve the sales. I included one equation, Einstein's famous $E = mc^2$. Maybe I would have sold twice as many copies without it."[2]

Read the following selection as quickly as possible and decide which title is the most appropriate. Write the title on the line.

1. Black Holes: Mysterious Powerhouses of the Universe

2. The Gravitational Force of Black Holes

3. Black Holes: Running Out of Fuel

4. Galaxies and Gravity

Black holes are among the most intriguing objects in the universe. Astronomers have used the words *mysterious* and *overwhelming* to describe these powerful objects in space. A black hole can be defined as a collapsed star that has become invisible. A black hole has such a strong gravitational force that nothing can escape from it, not even light. That is why a black hole is invisible: it traps light. Black holes have such strong gravity because they contain a tremendous amount of matter crushed into an incredibly tiny space. If the earth could be squeezed enough to become a black hole, it would be the size of a marble. Most astronomers believe the Milky Way Galaxy contains millions of black holes, though none has definitely been detected.

Astronomers believe that a black hole forms when a massive star runs out of nuclear fuel and is crushed by its own gravitational force. While a star burns fuel, it produces an outward push that counters the inward pull of gravity. When no more fuel remains, the internal pressure drops, and the star can no longer support its enormous weight. It throws off its outer layers in a gigantic explosion and its core collapses. Gravity can collapse a core measuring 10,000 miles (16,000 kilometers) in diameter into an object 10 miles in diameter in about one second. Astronomers are now able to predict many of the characteristics of black holes, and they continue to gather strong evidence for their existence. As technology advances, they hope to better understand the secrets of these powerhouses of the universe.[3]

Among the exciting, and often unexpected, discoveries to come out of research into space travel have been valuable earthly applications for many space products. In **Valuable By-Products of Space Research,** you will read about some of the many practical, everyday uses of these space-age products.

1. What practical benefits of space research can you think of? Make a list and share it with your classmates.

   _____

   _____

   _____

2. Do you think the benefits of space research outweigh the cost? Why or why not?

The article is organized around many examples of the practical applications of space research. As you read, underline the examples.

● ●

Valuable By-Products of Space Research

BY DAVID DOOLING AND

MITCHELL R. SHARPE

1   Research that went into developing the highly specialized technology for space travel has resulted in many unexpected practical applications back on earth. Out of the engineering that produced rocket motors, liquid propellants, space suits, and other necessities of space flight came by-products that no one had anticipated. Equipment and procedures designed for astronauts and space flights have been successfully adapted for use in medicine, industry, and the home. These valuable by-products of space research, called spin-offs, have improved the quality of life on earth in many ways.

New firefighter's suit
(similar to astronaut's)

2   Some of the best-known examples of spin-offs from space research are found in hospitals and doctors' offices. One such example is the sight switch, which was originally developed to allow astronauts to control their spacecraft without using their hands. The sight switch is now used by handicapped people to operate devices using eye movements. Another spin-off is the voice command device, which was designed to enable astronauts to steer their spacecraft by voice command. This device is now being used to help deaf people learn to speak.

3   Doctors have also benefited from the technology required to make miniature electronic instruments small enough and durable enough for trips into space. From this technology have come hearing aids the size of an aspirin and television cameras small enough to be attached to a surgeon's head to give medical students a close-up view of an operation.

4   Biotelemetry, which was developed to monitor the physical signs of astronauts by checking their temperature, brain-wave activity, breathing rate, and heartbeat, offers doctors a new means of monitoring hospital patients. Biosensors attached to the body send data by wire or radio. This information is displayed on terminals for doctors to analyze.

5   Aerospace scientists in England developed a special bed for astronauts that is now used for burn patients. It enables them to float on a cushion of air. The burns can heal more quickly because they do not rub against the bed.

6   Another valuable spin-off came from a special stretcher developed to remove injured workers from the huge propellant tanks of the *Saturn V* rocket. The stretcher is now widely employed to remove injured workers from mines, oil-drilling rigs, and boats. The rigid aluminum device permits someone to be moved through an opening eighteen inches in diameter.

7   Many items developed in space research are now being used in facto-

ries, offices, and homes. For example, fiberglass materials created for rocket-fuel tanks are used to make very strong and durable storage tanks, railway tank cars, and highway tankers. A magnetic hammer that originally served to eliminate small imperfections in the *Saturn V* rocket is being adapted for use in the automotive and shipbuilding industries.

8 One of the most valuable contributions of aerospace technology to industry is a management technique called the systems approach. With the aid of computers, this technique brings together all the elements of a complex project, including people, money, and materials, to assure that everything is completed at the optimum time. It has been applied to a variety of situations unrelated to space exploration. Among them are cancer research, hospital design, city planning, crime detection, pollution control, building construction, and transportation.

9 The experience gained from developing NASA spacesuits was applied to the process of designing clothing for use in other professions. Firefighters now have lighter, less bulky breathing apparatuses and special "fireblocking" materials that are more resistant to cracking and burning. Spacers used for ventilation and cushioning in moon boots were adapted for use in athletic shoes that are designed to reduce fatigue and injury.

● ●

HOW WELL DID YOU READ?

Circle the letter of the choice that best completes the sentence or answers the question.

1. The article mainly discusses _____ .

    a. devices that enable astronauts to control their spacecraft
    b. the value of the systems approach
    c. practical applications of space research
    d. ways of monitoring patients

2. The author mentions applications in all of the following areas except _____ .

    a. medicine
    b. industry
    c. the home
    d. the law

3. The author mentions hearing aids and television cameras as examples of _____ .

   a. spin-offs from the technology required to make miniature, durable instruments for space flight
   b. important applications of space research in industry
   c. inventions by aerospace scientists in England
   d. ways to enhance the benefits of the systems approach

4. The word *them* in paragraph 5 refers to _____ .

   a. aerospace scientists
   b. astronauts
   c. burn patients
   d. doctors

The Earth gets 100 tons heavier every day because of dust falling from space.

5. The word *such* in paragraph 2 refers to which of the following?

   a. spin-offs from space research
   b. research in hospitals
   c. research in doctors' offices
   d. handicapped people

6. Where in the article does the author mention ways to monitor a patient?

   a. paragraph 2
   b. paragraph 4
   c. paragraph 6
   d. paragraph 8

7. With what topic is paragraph 8 mainly concerned?

   a. the importance of management techniques
   b. the complexity of hospital design
   c. uses of computers in industry
   d. applications of the systems approach

8. The word *optimum* in paragraph 8 is closest in meaning to _____ .

   a. most accurate
   b. best
   c. latest
   d. fastest

Using the information that you underlined in the article, complete the chart.

Device	Space Use	Practical Application
Sight switch	lets astronauts control their spacecraft without using arms and legs	permits handicapped people to operate devices they could not otherwise use

EXPANDING VOCABULARY

SYNONYMS OR ANTONYMS

Decide if the following pairs of words are synonyms or antonyms. If they are synonyms, circle S. If they are antonyms, circle A.

1. spin-offs	by-products	S	A
2. device	implement	S	A
3. durable	sturdy	S	A
4. rigid	flexible	S	A
5. technique	method	S	A
6. trivial	significant	S	A
7. resistant	vulnerable	S	A
8. adapted	modified	S	A
9. reveals	conceals	S	A
10. allocate	assign	S	A

TALK IT OVER

DISCUSSION QUESTIONS

1. Have you ever used any of the devices mentioned in the article? If so, describe when and why.

2. Can you think of any instances when a spin-off has become more important than its originally intended purpose? If so, what are they?

3. Think of a question you would like to ask your classmates to generate discussion.

Many people feel that there is a wall dividing the worlds of art and science. In their minds, artists and scientists are very different types of people. Physicist Steve Huber is someone who doesn't fit the stereotype. In this interview, **Dancing to the Music of Physics,** Dr. Huber talks about the connection between art and science.

BEFORE YOU READ

PREREADING DISCUSSION

1. How would you describe a typical artist? Make a list of the adjectives that come to your mind when you think of an artist.

_____

_____

_____

_____

_____

_____

2. What is your impression of a typical scientist? Make a list of adjectives that you would use to describe a scientist.

_____

_____

_____

_____

_____

_____

3. Do you think that art and science are very different disciplines? How are they different?

4. Can you think of any ways that art and science are similar?

Dancing to the Music of Physics

DR. STEVE HUBER is an Associate Professor of Physics at Beaver College and an accomplished musician. As an undergraduate student he had two majors—physics and music. He also holds a Ph.D. in theoretical physics from Drexel University in Philadelphia, Pennsylvania. Dr. Huber worked his way through graduate school as a rehearsal pianist for several ballet companies. At age 23, he began to study dance and after several years of intense training, he performed professionally for a short time with Ballet Elan. Subsequently, he continued as a guest artist for a variety of other ballet companies while doing research in theoretical physics.

When did you first become interested in physics and music?

1   I can't remember a time when I wasn't interested in physics. When I was a child, I was very curious about the world around me. For example, I always wondered why light behaves the way it does. I found it more fun to play with a prism than to play with the kids in the neighborhood. I wasn't very social, but I was really into figuring out how things worked. I got my own telescope when I was eight years old, and I loved to take it out at night and go star gazing. I would look at the planets and stars and wonder what was out there. When I was ten, my father bought me a book on the universe, and I just ate it up. In fact, I still have that book right here in my office.

2   It was the same with music. I've always had a natural ear for music, perfect pitch. Even as a young child, if I heard a song on the radio, I could go right to the piano and play it. When I heard a sound like the ring of a telephone, I could identify its pitch and play the note on the piano. However, I didn't develop a serious interest in becoming a pianist until I was in college. I also seemed to do well in school in the visual arts like painting and drawing.

What commonality do you see between music and physics?

3   There is a common misconception that art and science are completely separate from each other. I think the distinction is artificial. In reality, art and science are not as mutually exclusive as one might assume. Solving a complicated mathematical problem, for example, can require the same degree of creative thinking as painting a landscape or writing a poem. I feel an indefinable tingle when I play the Schumann Concerto or dance the pas de deux from *Romeo and Juliet.* I get that same tingle from theoretical physics.

4   The beauty of art is readily apparent to most people. However, in the case of theoretical physics, the beauty is not nearly as accessible to the general

Assistant Professor of Physics, Dr. Steve Huber performs in a pas de deux from *Vivaldi's Concerto.*

public, but it is every bit as exciting. Nature seems to follow certain principles, very much the same as art does.

5   It's not uncommon for physicists to become accomplished musicians. Music theory is a very mathematical discipline. Relationships among various notes in classical harmony are based on simple mathematical relationships. For example, a note that is a perfect octave above another note is exactly twice the frequency of the original note. It took thousands of years for the musical scales to evolve into the major and minor scales that we have today. The relationship among the various notes in a scale is not arbitrary. What makes the sounds work together in harmony has precise mathematics behind it. This is true not only among notes in a chord, but with chord progressions as well. For example, there are very good technical reasons why a song may feel finished when it ends on one kind of chord, but feel unresolved when it ends on another kind.

You have said that physics is beautiful. What makes it beautiful to you?

6   To me, it's incredible the way nature seems to work so perfectly. I think it is beautiful. I always tell my students on the first day of class, "If you like reading Sherlock Holmes detective stories, you'll like doing physics problems." Physics is about figuring things out—discovering how they work, just like a detective.

7   A lot of people fear physics because they view it as a big complicated jumble of facts that have to be memorized. But that's not true, it's an understanding of how nature works, how the various parts interact. One can view art and literature as the relationships and interactions of ideas. Likewise, physics studies the relationships and interactions of concepts. In other words, to me art and science fundamentally attempt to achieve the same objective—an understanding of the world around us!

8   The whole universe seems to follow some very basic principles as it evolves in time. Some of these principles include the Conservation of Energy and the Conservation of Angular Momentum. The conservation laws of physics are analogous to non-interest bearing checking accounts. In the case of energy conservation, you can make energy deposits and energy withdrawals, but all the energy is accounted for.

9   The rotation of objects is governed by a law called the Conservation of Angular Momentum, which applies to everything in the universe including the rotation of stars, the rotation of the planets and their orbits, the behavior of an electron in an atom, the spin of a figure skater, and the rotation of wheels on a truck. What it all comes down to in the end is that everything in the universe fits together like the pieces of a perfect puzzle. As Einstein said, "The most incomprehensible thing about the universe is that it is comprehensible."

HOW WELL DID YOU READ?

Complete the following paragraph using information from the interview. Try to fill in as many blanks as you can without looking back at the text. You do not have to use the exact words from the interview as long as the idea is correct.

Dr. Steve Huber is _____ and _____ .

He believes that _____ and _____ are

_____ . According to Dr. Huber, both disciplines require

_____ . He also thinks that everything in

_____ is governed by _____ .

BUILDING READING SKILLS

UNDERSTANDING POINT OF VIEW

Put a check mark next to the statements you think Dr. Huber would agree with.

_____ 1. The beauty of physics is more accessible than the beauty of art.

_____ 2. Physics is more exciting than art.

_____ 3. The whole universe is governed by very basic principles.

_____ 4. Music is a very mathematical discipline.

_____ 5. Unlike art, physics attempts to understand the world around us.

TALK IT OVER

DISCUSSION QUESTIONS

1. Dr. Huber states that many people fear physics. Is this true for you? Why do you think that so many people are afraid of physics?

2. Do you believe that there is a wall dividing art and science? Are you or anyone you know interested in both art and science? Discuss the similarities between art and science in this context.

3. Have you ever read any Sherlock Holmes mysteries? Do you agree that they are like physics problems? Why or why not?

4. Do you agree with Einstein that the universe is comprehensible? Explain your answer.

5. Philosopher Will Durant wrote in 1926, "Every science begins as philosophy and ends as art." In what ways do you think Dr. Huber would agree with this idea?

BUILDING WRITING SKILLS

APPLICATION OF INFORMATION

Find an article on any aspect of science that interests you. Write a short summary of the main ideas of the article. Bring your summary and a copy of the article to share with your classmates.

A. Complete the chart by filling in the missing forms of the words. The adjective forms have been given.

VERB	NOUN	ADJECTIVE	ADVERB
		achievable	
		adjustable adjusted	
		applied applicable	
		conservative	
		considerable considerate	
		degenerative degenerated degenerating	
		evolved evolving evolutionary	
		identifiable identified	
		industrious industrial industrialized	
		observable observant	

B. Complete the sentences with words from the chart.

1. Some people do not believe in _____*evolution*_____ .

2. It took a _____ length of time to complete the project.

3. I have to _____ my watch. It's running several minutes fast.

4. Arthritis is a _____ disease that gets worse over time.

5. There have been many practical _____ of scientific discoveries resulting from space research.

6. The computer _____ has grown tremendously in the past decade.

7. Mr. Alden is very _____ in matters of finance and investment.

8. Elaine notices everything. She is a very _____ person.

9. The bank teller was able to _____ the thief with no trouble.

10. The article mentioned all of Dr. Friedman's _____ in the field of medicine.

POSTREADING

DISCUSSION
QUESTIONS

1. Science has been described as an endless frontier. Do you think this description is accurate? How would you describe science?

2. In defending the Skylab Space Program, Farouk El Baz wrote, "Man must have bread and butter, but he must also have something to lift his heart. The program is clean. We are not spending the money to kill people. We are not harming the environment. We are helping the spirit of man. We are unlocking secrets billions of years old."[4] What do you think are the pros and cons of costly space programs like Skylab?

3. In discussing life on other planets, Carl Sagan said, "Advanced civilizations—if they exist—aren't breaking their backs to save us before we destroy ourselves. Personally, I think that makes for a more interesting universe."[5] Do you agree with Sagan? Why or why not?

JUST FOR FUN

TOOTHPICK
TEASERS

Test yourself on these six toothpick puzzles. You'll need about fifteen toothpicks to solve the puzzles. Then check your answers on page 230 of the Answer Key. If you solved three, you're average. Four is good, five is excellent, and six makes you a genius!

1.

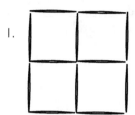

1. Change the positions of four toothpicks to make three small squares, all the same size, and no toothpicks left over.

2.

2. Change the positions of two toothpicks to make four small squares, all the same size, and no toothpicks left over.

3.

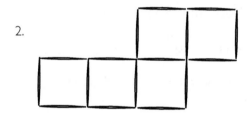

3. Remove six toothpicks completely, leaving ten on the table.

4.

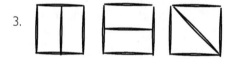

4. Move the position of one toothpick and make the house face east instead of west.

5.

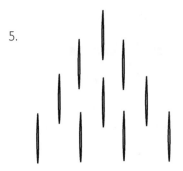

5. Change the positions of three toothpicks so that the triangular pattern points down instead of up.

6.

6. The picture shows how to make four triangles with nine toothpicks. Can you find a way to make four triangles with only six toothpicks? *Hint:* The solution to this toothpick teaser is different from the other five. It will require a completely new approach.

READER'S JOURNAL

Choose a topic that relates to the readings in this unit and write for about ten to twenty minutes. Consider writing about one of the quotes in this unit or answering one of the discussion questions.

READER'S JOURNAL

Date: _____

THE WORLD OF MARKETING

FYi

Unit·8

Selections

The presence of marketing can be felt in every field of business activity. Marketing includes everything that goes into researching, pricing, promoting, and distributing goods and services. Whenever you buy something, half of the money you spend goes to cover the cost of marketing. Marketing is important because it affects many aspects of your life. For example, the goods and services you buy, the stores you shop in, and the TV programs paid for by advertising are all available as a result of marketing efforts.

POINTS TO PONDER

DISCUSSION QUESTIONS

Think about and then discuss the following questions.

1. Make a list of some of your recent purchases. What kinds of things influenced your purchasing decisions? What are some factors you take into account when you buy something?

_____

_____

_____

_____

_____

2. In your opinion, is there a relationship between psychology and sales? If so, what is it?

3. Do you think there is a strong connection between culture and business? If so, how can this affect the way companies do business internationally? What kinds of cross-cultural problems might a company encounter when it does business in another country?

Advertisers have many different ways of promoting and selling their products. In **How to Analyze an Ad,** you will learn how to become a smarter consumer.

1. What kinds of ads do you like? Describe them and give some examples. What kinds of ads do you dislike? Why?

2. How are your purchasing decisions influenced by the ads you see, hear, or read?

3. Do you consider yourself to be an astute consumer? Why or why not?

How to Analyze an Ad

Advertisers use all kinds of strategies to get your attention and your dollars. By asking some basic questions, you can learn to cut through the hype.

By Phil Sudo

1 No one likes to be a sucker. If you don't pay attention, though, ads can make you one. You can protect yourself by learning how to analyze ads. Once you understand the strategies and techniques advertisers use—the buttons they're trying to push—you can spot attempts at manipulation and make better, more critical decisions about what's being advertised. You can even heighten your appreciation of ads—which ones you think are good and which ones you think are bad.

2 So the next time you notice an ad, ask yourself some of these questions:

What Kind of Ad Is It?

3   The majority of ads are called *product ads*—those intended to promote the millions of different goods and services for sale, from baking soda to banking. Other kinds of ads include: *corporate ads,* which promote a company's image or philosophy rather than a product; *political ads,* which aim to generate votes for a candidate or against an opponent; and *public-service ads,* which offer help, promote a cause, or seek donations.

What's the Target?

4   One reason we ignore so many ads is because they're not aimed at us. Advertisers seek to maximize an ad's effectiveness by identifying a *target market*—the audience they most want to reach. To do so, they divide the market into categories: by age, sex, income level, education, geographic region, ethnic background, political leaning, life-style—the list goes on and on. A maker of hockey sticks, for example, is going to target young males who live in cold-weather areas and take part in sports. Thus, its hockey-stick ads would be tailored to appeal to the likes and desires of that market alone.

5   A company with a wide target audience, like McDonald's, will develop several different ads, each aimed at a specific segment of the market—one for teenagers, one in Spanish, one for black families. It may cost more than having a single ad designed for everybody, but it is a more calculated, direct method of selling.

Where Is the Ad Found?

6   It makes no sense for the seller of arthritis medication to run an ad on MTV, or for a skateboard maker to advertise on *Oprah.* Advertisers seek to place their ads in media viewed by their target audience. A public-safety department, for example, might put a billboard about seat belts near a site where accidents are high. Similarly, a ritzy mail-order house might send its catalogues only to ZIP codes like 90210 and other high-income areas.

What Is the Sales Pitch?

7   The foundation of an ad is the sales pitch. To make the pitch, ads play on our needs and desires—those basic, often instinctive forces that motivate us to do something. Says one corporate marketing director, "Fear, envy, vanity, health, utility, profit, pride, love, and entertainment. If you ever spend money, it will be for one of those reasons." Here is where your guard should go up. If you can identify the buttons an ad is trying to push, you can avoid manipulation.

What Is the Subtext?

8   All ads have a *subtext*—that is, a meaning beneath the surface. The subtext of an ad is often what causes the most controversy, usually for fostering sexism or racial and ethnic stereotypes. Ads for laundry detergent, for example, are sometimes criticized for portraying women only as housewives.

9   By looking at the deeper level of ads, you can critique not only the attitudes of the advertiser, but our culture at large—what we value, how we see ourselves. With that knowledge, you can buy into those values or not. At least you'll know you're not getting suckered.

Ad It Up, Break It Down

How savvy are you when it comes to looking at ads? Here are three magazine ads for you to analyze. Look at each one, then read the text that accompanies it. When you're done, use the questions at the end for classroom discussion. What other insights can you bring to these ads? –H.B.

Diesel Jeans in *Spin* Magazine

What it says: "How to teach your children to love and care. Modern children need to solve their own problems: teaching kids to kill helps them deal directly with reality—but they learn so much quicker when you give them a guiding hand! Make them proud and confident! Man, if they never learn to blast the brains out of their neighbors what kind of damn future has this country of ours got???"

What it means: As urban kids have increasingly turned to guns to be cool, so have advertisers.

Many teen-oriented ads today feature firearms, alarming critics who see it as glorifying guns and violence. This ad tries to have it both ways–visually showing a "cool guy" with a gun, then using the text to make fun of violence in society. The woman in the ad could be a target, or the "modern child" referred to in the text.

What do you think? What's the target market for this ad? What links does it make between guns and fashion? Do ads like this contribute to violence in society, or defuse it? How does it portray women?

Esprit Junior Sportswear in *Sassy* and *Glamour*

What it says: "Esprit" over a model's flower-painted face.

What it means: This ad assumes familiarity with the Esprit brand name, because it doesn't show any products. According to Esprit officials, the face paint is a reference to the "flower power" era of the 1970s, which the company's new clothing styles are emphasizing.

The ad is notable for using a black model. Although the appearance of black and ethnic models is on the rise in mainstream magazines, few have been signed to lucrative contracts with cosmetics companies. Most companies still favor white models because their target market is white. Critics say that over the years, advertisers have created a mainstream ideal of beauty that is white, subtly telling minorities that they don't meet the standard.

What do you think? What's the target market for this ad? How is the ad supposed to help Esprit's sales? Does the model's skin color affect how you view the ad? What effect do ads have on society's notions of beauty?

Bari-Jay Dresses in *YM* (formerly *Young Miss*)

What it says: "Supermodel prom," the opening page of a five-page photo spread on what to wear to the prom.

What it means: Technically, this is not an advertisement. According to *YM,* advertisers don't pay to have their merchandise featured in photo layouts. (Some publications solicit ads by promising feature articles if companies will buy ad space.) But in the corner text, the magazine lists the brand of the products, the prices, and where to buy them. And it describes the dress as something to "blow the competition off the dance floor." Some people believe fashion layouts like these blur the line between advertising and editorial opinion.

What do you think? What is the difference between this article and an ad? Does this article have more credibility than an ad? Would you, as an advertiser, threaten to pull your ads to pressure an editor's decision? Would you, as an editor, ever write something critical about a product made by one of your advertisers?

EXPANDING VOCABULARY

DEFINING TERMS

It is important to be able to recognize when a term is defined in the text. Sometimes an author will explain a word by putting the definition in parentheses, after a dash, or in a relative clause. Find the following words in the article and write a definition for each one.

1. product ads (¶3) _____

_____

_____

2. corporate ads (¶3) _____

_____

_____

3. political ads (¶3) _____

_____

_____

4. public-service ads (¶3) _____

_____

_____

5. target market (¶4) _____

_____

_____

6. sales pitch (¶7) _____

_____

_____

7. subtext (¶8) _____

_____

_____

The largest employer in the world is Indian Railways with over 1,654,066 employees.

BUILDING READING SKILLS

MAKING INFERENCES

An **inference** is a reasonable conclusion that we make based on information that we have. It is an educated guess. Good readers are constantly making inferences based on the information provided in the text.

Read the following statements. Put a check mark next to the statements you can infer from information in the article.

_____ 1. By learning how to analyze ads, you can avoid being a sucker.

_____ 2. Advertisers try to manipulate your decisions.

_____ 3. There are fewer political ads than corporate ads.

_____ 4. Coca Cola has different ads aimed at different segments of the market.

_____ 5. It is possible to learn something about the values of a culture from its ads.

_____ 6. MTV is not a good place to run ads for older people.

_____ 7. Advertisers can use zip codes to identify certain types of target markets.

_____ 8. Most people who eat at McDonald's are teenagers.

APPLICATION OF INFORMATION

ANALYZING SUBTEXTS

1. According to the author, the subtext of many ads can be controversial. Some ads seem to promote sexism and racism. Others encourage ethnic stereotyping. Look through some magazines for ads with controversial subtexts. Cut them out and bring them to class. Be prepared to explain the subtexts of the ads and what they show.

2. The subtext of an ad can also give clues about the values of a culture. Some American values that ads try to show include the importance of family life, planning for the future, hard work, looking young, cleanliness, and getting your money's worth. Look for ads that express some of these values and bring them to class.

3. Choose one of the following topics and prepare a short presentation.
   a. Advertisements are a reflection of society.
   b. Advertisements are a powerful tool that can change society.
   c. Advertising in the United States is different from advertising in my native country.
   d. We are manipulated by advertisements.

The following two articles deal with various aspects of international business. The first one, **Do's and Taboos: Cultural Aspects of International Business,** focuses on cultural differences that can affect all areas of international business practices and decisions. The second article, **Big Blunders from Big Business,** deals more specifically with the marketing and advertising problems that can arise when companies try to sell their products abroad.

BEFORE YOU READ

1. A **taboo** is something that is forbidden according to custom. Discuss the concept of taboos in your culture. What examples of taboos you can think of?

2. Look through the article and read the five callouts in bold print in the margin. From these, make some predictions about the kinds of things the author might discuss in the article.

_____

_____

_____

_____

● ●

Do's and Taboos

CULTURAL ASPECTS OF INTERNATIONAL BUSINESS

BY M. KATHERINE GLOVER

WRITER, *BUSINESS AMERICA*

INTERNATIONAL TRADE ADMINISTRATION

1 Never touch the head of a Thai or pass an object over it, as the head is considered sacred in Thailand. Likewise, never point the bottoms of the feet in the direction of another person in Thailand or cross your legs while sitting, especially in the presence of an older person.

2 Avoid using triangular shapes in Hong Kong, Korea, or Taiwan, as the triangle is considered a negative shape in those countries.

3 Remember that the number 7 is considered bad luck in Kenya, good luck in Czechoslovakia, and has magical connotations in Benin.

4   Red is a positive color in Denmark, but represents witchcraft and death in many African countries.

5   A nod means "no" in Bulgaria, and shaking the head side-to-side means "yes."

6   Understanding and heeding cultural variables such as these is one of the most significant aspects of being successful in any international business endeavor. A lack of familiarity with the business practices, social customs, and etiquette of a country can weaken a company's position in the market, prevent it from accomplishing its objectives, and ultimately lead to failure.

7   As business has become increasingly international and communications technology continues to develop, the need for clearly understood communication between members of different cultures is even more crucial.

8   Growing competition for international markets is another reason that companies must consider cultural distinctions. As Secretary of Commerce Robert Mosbacher indicated, "American companies have to rely on all available tactics for winning in the global marketplace today. Learning international business diplomacy should be the first step they take."

9   Business executives who are not alert to cultural differences simply cannot function efficiently overseas. They may not even understand something as basic as what signifies closing a deal in a particular country—a handshake, a written contract, or a memorandum of understanding.

10   Taking the time to learn something about the culture of a country before doing business there is also a show of respect and is usually deeply appreciated, not to mention rewarding for the company. Those who understand the culture are more likely to develop successful, long-term business relationships.

11   Customs vary widely from one country to another. Something with one meaning in one area may mean the opposite somewhere else. Some of the cultural distinctions that firms most often face include differences in business styles, attitudes towards development of business relationships, attitudes towards punctuality, negotiating styles, gift-giving customs, greetings, significance of gestures, meanings of colors and numbers, and customs regarding titles.

12   American firms must pay close attention to different styles of doing business and the degree of importance placed on developing business relationships. In some countries, business people have a very direct style, while in others they are much more subtle in style. Many nationalities value the personal relationship more than most Americans do in business. In these countries, long-term relationships based on trust are necessary for doing business. Many U.S. firms make the mistake of rushing into business discussions and "coming on too strong" instead of nurturing the relationship first. According to Roger Axtell in his book *Do's and Taboos of Hosting International Visitors,* "There is much more to business than just business in many parts of the world. Socializing, friendships, etiquette, grace, patience, and protocol are integral parts of business. Jumping right into business discussions before a get-acquainted interlude can be a bad mistake."

13   Charles Ford, Commercial Attaché in Guatemala, cites this cultural distinction as the greatest area of difference between the American and

> Adapting to culture variables is a significant part of any international business endeavor.

Guatemalan styles of doing business. The inexperienced American visitor, he claims, often tries to force a business relationship. The abrupt "always watching the clock" style rarely works in Guatemala. A better informed business executive would, he advises, engage in small talk about Guatemala, indicate an interest in the families of his or her business associates, join them for lunch or dinner, and generally allow time for a personal relationship to develop. Solid business opportunities usually follow a strong personal relationship in Guatemala. This holds true for Latin America in general.

14   Building a personal rapport is also important when doing business in Greece, according to Sondra Snowdon, President of Snowdon's International Protocol, Inc., a firm that trains and prepares executives in cross-cultural communications. Business entertaining is usually done in the evening at a local taverna, and spouses are often included. The relaxed atmosphere is important to building a business relationship based on friendship.

15   Belgians, however, are the opposite, Snowdon says. They are likely to get down to business right away and are unusually conservative and efficient in their approach to business meetings.

16   Attitudes toward punctuality vary greatly from one culture to another and unless understood can cause confusion and misunderstanding. Romanians, Japanese, and Germans are very punctual, while many of the Latin countries have a more relaxed attitude toward time. The Japanese consider it rude to be late for a business meeting, but it is acceptable, even fashionable, to be late for a social occasion.

Learning about a country's culture is a show of respect and is always appreciated.

17   In Guatemala on the other hand, according to Ford, a luncheon at a specified time means that some guests might be 10 minutes early, while others may be 45 minutes late.

18   When crossing cultural lines, something as simple as a greeting can be misunderstood. The form of greeting differs from culture to culture. Traditional greetings may be a handshake, hug, nose rub, kiss, placing the hands in praying position, or various other gestures. Lack of awareness concerning the country's accepted form of greeting can lead to awkward encounters.

19   The Japanese bow is one of the most well-known forms of greeting. The bow symbolizes respect and humility and is a very important custom to observe when doing business with the Japanese. There are also different levels of bowing, each with a significant meaning. Japanese and Americans often combine a handshake with a bow so that each culture may show the other respect.

20   Handshakes are the accepted form of greeting in Italy. Italians use a handshake for greetings and goodbyes. Unlike the United States, men do not stand when a woman enters or leaves a room, and they do not kiss a woman's hand. The latter is reserved for royalty.

21   The traditional Thai greeting, the wai, is made by placing both hands together in a prayer position at the chin and bowing slightly. The higher the hands, the more respect is symbolized. The fingertips should never be raised above eye level. The gesture means "thank you" and "I'm sorry" as well as "hello." Failure to return a wai greeting is equivalent to refusing to shake hands in the West.

22   According to Snowdon, American intentions are often misunderstood and Americans are sometimes perceived as not meaning what they say.

The traditional Thai greeting, the wai.

For example, in Denmark the standard American greeting "Hi, how are you?" leads the Danes to think the U.S. business person really wants to know how they are. She suggests that, "Hi, I'm pleased to meet you" is preferable and conveys a more sincere message.

23   People around the world use body movements or gestures to convey specific messages. Though countries sometimes use the same gestures, they often have very different meanings. Misunderstandings over gestures is a common occurrence in cross-cultural communication, and misinterpretation along these lines can lead to business complications and social embarrassment.

24   The "OK" sign commonly used in the United States is a good example of a gesture that has several different meanings according to the country. In France, it means zero; in Japan, it is a symbol for money; and in Brazil, it carries a vulgar connotation.

25   Assistant Commercial Attaché in the United Kingdom Thomas Kelsey advises that American businessmen should never sit with the ankle resting on the knee. They should instead cross their legs with one knee on top of the other. He also suggests avoiding backslapping and putting an arm around a new acquaintance.

26   In Thailand, it is considered offensive to place one's arm over the back of the chair in which another person is sitting, and men and women should not show affection in public.

27   The use of a palm-up hand and moving index finger signals "come here" in the United States and in some other countries but is considered vulgar in others. In Ethiopia, holding out the hand palm down and repeatedly closing the hand means "come here."

28   Proper use of names and titles is often a source of confusion in international business relations. In many countries (including the United Kingdom, France, and Denmark), it is appropriate to use titles until use of first names is suggested.

29   First names are seldom used when doing business in Germany. Visiting business people should use the surname preceded by the title. Titles such as "Herr Direktor" are sometimes used to indicate prestige, status, and rank.

30   Thais, on the other hand, address each other by first names and reserve last names for very formal occasions, or in writing. When using the first name, they often use the honorific "Khun" or a title preceding it. In Belgium, it is important to address French-speaking business contacts as "Monsieur" or "Madame," while Dutch-speaking contacts should be addressed as "Mr." or "Mrs." According to Sondra Snowdon, to confuse the two is a great insult.

> When crossing cultural lines something as simple as a greeting can be misunderstood.

31 Customs concerning gift-giving are extremely important to understand. In some cultures, gifts are expected, and failure to present them is considered an insult, whereas in other countries, offering a gift is considered offensive. Business executives also need to know when to present gifts—on the initial visit or afterwards; where to present gifts—in public or private; what type of gift to present; what color it should be; and how many to present.

32 Gift-giving is an important part of doing business in Japan. Exchanging gifts symbolizes the depth and strength of a business relationship to the Japanese. Gifts are usually exchanged at the first meeting. When presented with a gift, companies are expected to respond by giving a gift.

33 In sharp contrast, gifts are rarely exchanged in Germany and are usually not appropriate. Small gifts are fine, but expensive items are not a general practice.

34 Gift-giving is not a normal custom in Belgium or the United Kingdom either, although in both countries, flowers are a suitable gift if invited to someone's home. Even that is not as easy as it sounds. International executives must use caution to choose appropriate flowers. For example, avoid sending chrysanthemums (especially white) in Belgium and elsewhere in Europe since they are mainly used for funerals. In Europe, it is also considered bad luck to present an even number of flowers. Beware of white flowers in Japan where they are associated with death, and purple flowers in Mexico and Brazil.

35 Yue-Sai Kan, host and executive producer of a television show about Asia—*Looking East*—and of a new four-part series on *Doing Business in Asia,* points out that customs toward the exchange of business cards vary, too. Seemingly minor in importance, observance of a country's customs towards card-giving is a key part of business protocol.

36 In Japan, it is particularly important to be aware of the way business cards should be exchanged, according to Yue-Sai Kan. The western tradition of accepting a business card and immediately putting it in your pocket is considered very rude there, she contends. The proper approach is to carefully look at the card after accepting it, observe the title and organization, acknowledge with a nod that you have digested the information, and perhaps make a relevant comment or ask a polite question. During a meeting, spread the cards in front of you relating to where people are sitting. In other words says Yue-Sai Kan, treat a business card as you would treat its owner—with respect.

37 When presenting a card in either Japan or South Korea, it is important to use both hands and position the card so that the recipient can read it. In any country where English is not commonly taught, the data should be printed in the native language on the reverse side of the card.

38 Negotiating can be a complex process between parties from the same nation. Negotiating across cultures is even more complicated because of the added chance of misunderstanding stemming from cultural differences. Negotiating styles differ from nation to nation. In addition, a host of cultural variables must be dealt with all at once.

39 For example, it is essential to understand the importance of rank in the other country and to know who the decision makers are. It is equally

important to be familiar with the business style of the foreign company. Is it important to be direct or subtle? Is it necessary to have an established relationship with the company before beginning negotiations? Executives negotiating with foreign companies must also understand the nature of agreements in the country, the significance of gestures, and negotiating etiquette.

40   These cultural variables are examples of the things that U.S. executives involved in international business must be aware of. At times in the past, Americans have not had a good track record of being sensitive to cultural distinctions. However, as business has become more global, Americans have become more sensitive to cultural differences and the importance of dealing with them effectively. Still, some companies fail to do their homework and make fatal or near-fatal mistakes that could have easily been prevented. A number of firms have learned the hard way that successful domestic strategies do not necessarily work overseas and that business must be adapted to the culture.

41   Failure to research and understand a culture before entering the market has led to many international business blunders. They run the gamut from forgivable to disastrous. Some years ago, for example, a leading U.S. golf ball manufacturer targeted Japan as an important new market for golf. However, sales of the company's golf balls were well below average. The firm, as it turned out, had packaged the balls in groups of four—the number of death in Japan.

42   David Ricks, in his book *Big Business Blunders: Mistakes in Multinational Marketing,* cites a number of other blunders that resulted from cultural oversights. One concerns a telephone company that tried to incorporate a Latin flavor in its commercial by employing Puerto Rican actors. In the ad, the wife said to her husband, "Run downstairs and phone Mary. Tell her we'll be a little late." The commercial contained two major cultural errors: Latin wives seldom dare order their husbands around, and almost no Latin would feel it necessary to phone to warn of tardiness since it is expected.

43   Another company experienced headaches caused by poor translation. A Mexican magazine promotion for an American-brand shirt carried a message stating the opposite of what had originally been intended. The advertisement, instead of reading "when I used this shirt, I felt good," said "until I used this shirt, I felt good."

44   A toothpaste company tried to sell its product in regions of Southeast Asia through a promotion which stressed that the toothpaste helped enhance white teeth. In this area, where some local people deliberately chewed betel nut in order to achieve the social prestige of darkly stained teeth, such an ad was less than effective. The slogan "wonder where the yellow went" was also viewed as a racial slur.

45   Mistakes of these types can at the least reduce sales, and at the worst, give the company and the product such a bad name that it closes out the market entirely. To avoid blunders like this, a company ultimately must not only have a sensitivity to other cultures but also must have a good understanding of its own culture and how other countries see American culture.

Failure to research and understand a culture has led to many international business blunders.

BUILDING READING SKILLS

SCANNING FOR SUPPORTING EXAMPLES

Scanning is a quick way to locate specific information in a passage. Scanning is different from reading. When you scan, you move your eyes very quickly across and down the page with one purpose: to find the information you need.

Scan the article to find specific examples to support the following generalizations. Complete the chart below.

Numbers have different meanings around the world.
Colors have different connotations in different countries.
Shapes do not always mean the same thing everywhere.
The style of doing business varies from country to country.
Attitudes toward punctuality differ from one place to another.
Even something as simple as a greeting can be misunderstood.
People around the world use different gestures and body movements to convey specific meanings.
Proper use of names and titles is often a source of confusion in international business relations.
Gift-giving customs in other countries require careful attention.

Decide if the following pairs of words are synonyms or antonyms. If they are synonyms, circle S. If they are antonyms, circle A.

1. connotation	implication	S	A
2. subtle	direct	S	A
3. crucial	unimportant	S	A
4. abrupt	gradual	S	A
5. punctual	late	S	A
6. etiquette	protocol	S	A
7. suitable	appropriate	S	A
8. contend	claim	S	A
9. incorporate	exclude	S	A
10. deliberately	intentionally	S	A

Choose five words from this article that are new to you and teach them to your classmates. Present a definition for each word and a sentence that uses the word.

1. _____

_____

2. _____

_____

3. _____

_____

4. _____

_____

5. _____

_____

The first rule of advertising is know your target market. This is especially true in today's global marketplace where cultural differences come into play. In **Big Blunders from Big Business,** you will read about several instances in which marketers failed to follow that rule and the sometimes humorous, but always costly, consequences.

1. Look at the cartoon and discuss why it is funny.

WE TAKE YOUR BAGS AND SEND THEM IN ALL DIRECTIONS!

fig. 8.4

2. Misunderstandings often result from trying to communicate in a foreign language. Have you ever tried to express something in another language that resulted in a misunderstanding? Was it funny? embarrassing? frustrating? If so, share your story with the rest of the class.

In Unit 3 you learned some important previewing techniques. These techniques are especially helpful in dealing with a longer article. If you are familiar with the basic content and the organization of the text, you will have more control over what you are reading.

Before you read "Big Blunders from Big Business," you should spend a few minutes previewing the article. Follow the steps below.

1. Look at the title and think about what it means. Read the subtitle and try to guess what kinds of mistakes the author is referring to. Consider what you already know about the topic. Do you have any opinions about it?

2. Look through the article and read the headings. Try to guess what each section will be about.

(continued on the next page)

3. Look at the picture. Think about what it means and why the author included it.

4. Read the first paragraph and determine the tone of the article. What ideas are introduced in the beginning of the article? How do you think the author might develop them?

5. Skim the last two paragraphs. What conclusions do you think the author is making?

6. Read the first sentence of every paragraph. Try to guess the main ideas of the article.

7. Read the whole article one time quickly without stopping. Do not worry about details or words that you do not know. You are just reading for a general idea.

8. Write a few sentences that predict what you think the article will be about.

_____

_____

_____

Now read the whole article and do the exercises that follow.

● ●

Big Blunders from Big Business

MISTAKES IN GLOBAL MARKETING CAN BE EMBARRASSING AND COSTLY

1　International marketing can be a tricky business. With the increase in global trade, international companies cannot afford to make costly advertising mistakes if they want to be competitive and profitable. Understanding the language and culture of target markets in foreign countries is one of the keys to successful international marketing. Too many companies, however, have jumped into foreign markets with embarrassing results. Out of their blunders, a whole new industry of translation services has emerged.

Ads for American products can show up in the most unlikely places, like this little café in a remote Moroccan village.

FAULTY TRANSLATIONS

2 The value of understanding the language of a country cannot be overestimated. Translation mistakes are at the heart of many blunders in international advertising. Since a language is more than the sum of its words, a literal, word-by-word dictionary translation seldom works. The following examples prove this point. Otis Engineering Company once displayed a poster at a trade show in Moscow that turned heads. Due to a poor translation of its message, the sign boasted that the firm's equipment was great for improving a person's sex life. The Parker Pen Company suffered an embarrassing moment when it realized that a faulty translation of one of its ads into Spanish resulted in a promise to "help prevent unwanted pregnancies."

3 Automobile manufacturers in the United States have made several notorious advertising mistakes that have been well publicized. General Motors learned a costly lesson when it introduced its Chevrolet Nova to the Puerto Rican market. Although "nova" means "star" in Spanish, when it is spoken, it sounds like "no va" which means "it doesn't go." Few people wanted to buy a car with that meaning. When GM changed the name to Caribe, sales picked up dramatically. Ford also ran into trouble with the name of one of its products. When it introduced a low-cost truck called the "Fiera" into Spanish-speaking countries, Ford didn't realize until too late that the name meant "ugly old woman" in Spanish. Another American auto manufacturer made a mistake when it translated its Venezuelan ad for a car battery. It was no surprise when Venezuelan customers didn't want to buy a battery that was advertised as being "highly overrated."

4 Airline companies have also experienced problems of poor translation. A word-by-word translation ruined a whole advertising campaign for Braniff Airlines. Hoping to promote its plush leather seats, Braniff's ad urged passengers to "fly on leather." However, when the slogan was translated into Spanish, it told customers to "fly naked." Another airline company, Eastern Airlines, made a similar mistake when it translated its motto, "We earn our wings daily" into Spanish. The poor translation suggested that its passengers often ended up dead.

5 Marketing blunders have also been made by food and beverage companies. One American food company's friendly "Jolly Green Giant" became something quite different when it was translated into Arabic as "Intimidating Green Ogre." When translated into German, Pepsi's popular slogan, "Come Alive with Pepsi" came out implying "Come Alive from the Grave." No wonder customers in Germany didn't rush out to buy Pepsi. Even a company with an excellent international track record like Kentucky Fried Chicken is not immune to the perils of faulty translation. A lot of sales were lost when the catch phrase "finger lickin' good" became "eat your fingers off" in the Chinese translation.

6   A manufacturer of one laundry detergent made an expensive mistake in a promotional campaign in the Middle East. The advertisements showed a picture of a pile of dirty clothes on the left, a box of the company's detergent in the middle, and clean clothes on the right. Unfortunately, the message was incorrectly interpreted because most people in the Middle East read from right to left. It seemed to them that the detergent turned clean clothes into dirty ones.

CULTURAL OVERSIGHTS CAN BE DISASTROUS

7   Successful international marketing doesn't stop with good translations—other aspects of culture must be researched and understood if marketers are to avoid blunders. When marketers do not understand and appreciate the values, tastes, geography, climate, superstitions, level of literacy, religion, or economic development of a culture, they fail to capture their target market. For example, when a popular American designer tried to introduce a new perfume in the Latin American market, the product aroused little interest and the company lost a lot of money. Ads for the new fragrance highlighted its fresh camellia scent. What marketers had failed to realize was that camellias are traditionally used for funerals in many South American countries.

8   Procter and Gamble has been successful in marketing its products internationally for many years. Today, overseas markets account for over one third of its sales. However, the company's success in this area didn't happen overnight. Procter and Gamble initially experienced huge losses because marketing managers did not recognize important cultural differences. For instance, when P&G first entered the Japanese market with its popular Cheer laundry detergent, most Japanese housewives weren't interested. The promotional campaign that emphasized Cheer as an effective "all temperature" detergent was lost on the Japanese who usually wash clothes in cold water. Although the pitch had been quite successful in the United States where clothes are washed in all temperatures, it fell flat in Japan. All of this could have been avoided if P&G marketers had done more preliminary research before launching the campaign. Once P&G changed its strategy and promised superior cleaning in cold water, sales for Cheer picked up dramatically.

9   The use of numbers can also be a source of problems for international marketers. Since every culture has its own set of lucky and unlucky numbers, companies need to do their homework if they want to avoid marketing blunders. A U.S. manufacturer of golf balls learned this lesson the hard way when it packaged its product in groups of four for export to Japan. The company couldn't figure out why the golf balls weren't selling well until it realized that in Japanese the word for the number four also means death. In Japan four and nine are very unlucky numbers which should be avoided by marketers.

10   Even illustrations need to be carefully examined. A picture that is culturally offensive can ruin an advertisement even if the written message is properly translated. McDonnell Douglas Corporation made an unfortunate error in an aircraft brochure for potential customers in India. It included a picture of men wearing turbans, which was not appreciated by the Indians. A company spokesman reported, "It was politely pointed out to us that turbans were distinctly Pakistani Moslem." The artist for the ad had used an old National Geographic magazine to copy the picture.

PREVENTING BLUNDERS

11   Having awakened to the special nature of foreign advertising, companies are becoming much more conscientious in securing accurate translations. They are also becoming much more sensitive to the cultural distinctions and variables that play such an important role in any international business venture. Above all, the best way to guard against errors is to hire trained professional translators who thoroughly understand the target language and its idiomatic usage. These translators should be very familiar with the culture and people of the country, and have a grasp of the technical aspects of the industry.

12   Many international companies are using a technique called "backtranslation," which greatly reduces the possibility of advertising blunders. The process of backtranslation requires one person to translate the message into the target language and another person to translate the new version back into the original language. The purpose is to determine whether the original material and the retranslated material are the same. In this way companies can ensure that their intended message is really being conveyed.

13   Effective translators aim to capture the overall message of an advertisement because a word-for-word duplication of the original rarely conveys the intended meaning and often causes misunderstandings. In designing advertisements to be used in other countries, marketers are recognizing the need to keep messages as short and simple as possible and to avoid idioms, jargon, and slang that are difficult to translate. Similarly, they avoid jokes, since humor does not translate well from one culture to another. What is considered funny in one part of the world may not be so humorous in another. The bottom line is that consumers interpret advertising in terms of their own cultures. As the global marketplace opens up, there is no room for linguistic or cultural blunders.[1]

● ●

HOW WELL DID YOU READ?

In small groups, identify the reasons that each of the following advertising campaigns failed.

1. General Motor's Chevrolet Nova in Puerto Rico

   _____

   _____

2. Braniff Airline's promotion for leather seats in Spanish-speaking countries

   _____

   _____

3. Kentucky Fried Chicken's advertisement in China

   _____

   _____

(continued on the next page)

213

4. an American laundry detergent ad in the Middle East

_____

_____

5. an American designer's perfume campaign in South America

_____

_____

6. Procter and Gamble's ad for Cheer in Japan

_____

_____

7. an American company's packaging of golf balls for export to Japan

_____

_____

8. McDonnell Douglas Corporation's brochure for India

_____

_____

FIGURE IT OUT
IDIOMS

Using the context of the sentence, write a definition for the highlighted expressions.

1. *Translation mistakes are **at the heart of** many blunders in international marketing.*

_____

2. *Otis Engineering Company once displayed a poster at a trade show in Moscow that **turned heads.***

_____

3. *Ford also **ran into** trouble with the name of one of its products.*

_____

4. *Even a company with an excellent international* **track record** *like Kentucky Fried Chicken is not immune to the perils of faulty translation.*

_____

5. *A lot of sales were lost when the* **catch phrase** *"finger lickin good" became "eat your fingers off" in Chinese.*

_____

6. *The promotional campaign that emphasized Cheer as an effective "all temperature" detergent was* **lost on** *the Japanese who usually wash clothes in cold water.*

_____

7. *Although the pitch had been quite successful in the United States where clothes are washed in all temperatures, it* **fell flat** *in Japan.*

_____

8. *Once P&G changed its strategy and promised superior cleaning in cold water, sales for Cheer* **picked up** *dramatically.*

_____

9. ***The bottom line*** *is that consumers interpret advertising in terms of their own cultures.*

_____

TALK IT OVER

DISCUSSION
QUESTIONS

Write five discussion questions for your classmates to answer based on issues raised in "Do's and Taboos" and "Big Blunders from Big Business." Then discuss the answers in small groups.

1. _____

2. _____

3. _____

4. _____

5. _____

Read the following selection as quickly as possible and decide which title is the most appropriate. Write the title on the line.

1. Colors Communicate

2. Green and Purple: A Sign of Religious Leadership

3. An Expensive Lesson in Malaysia

4. The Westernization of Asia

Hong Kong is a city inclined toward red; in Thailand the color is yellow; India leans toward reds and oranges. These are not political colors, but colors that connote religious beliefs.

To an Asian colors are infused with beliefs, religious and otherwise. To the Chinese, red is very lucky, but to Thais yellow brings good fortune. The combination of blue, black, and white is, to the Chinese, suggestive of a funeral.

Many Western businessmen believe that most Asians have become Westernized in their outlook. This is true in part. But Westernization and education do not usually completely replace the culture and beliefs of an Asian's forefathers. They tend instead to make a more intricate alliance between his culture and religious bonds. The approach required to sell an Asian any commodity must follow the basic formula of catering to national pride, acknowledging equality, and understanding the Asian's beliefs.

Color is a touchy thing. Advertisers are advised to take into consideration the religious and superstitious beliefs connected with colors before using them. The color combinations of green and purple are acceptable throughout Asia as these colors seem to have been worn by religious leaders in earlier times.

However, using one or both of these colors is no guarantee of sales, as a prominent manufacturer of water-recreation products learned in Malaysia. Its home office received heated requests from its Malaysian distributors to stop shipments on all products colored green. The distributors reported that numerous customers associated the color green with the jungle and illness![2]

In the world of advertising, it is sometimes difficult to separate fantasy from reality. **Style's Hidden Persuaders** discusses several people, called stylists, whose job it is to keep the image of fantasy real. Behind the scenes of TV, movies, and advertisements, stylists and costumers work hard to create and sell the images we see.

1. How influenced are you by the fashions you see in movies, on TV, and in advertisements?

2. Are you an image-conscious person? In what ways?

Style's Hidden Persuaders

BY JENNET CONANT

Behind the lights of TV, movies and ads, costumers and stylists shop till they drop to soft-sell alluring looks we want to watch and wear.

1   Patrick Norris is a costume supervisor for the yuppie TV chronicle *thirtysomething*. Norris is a member of an unseen but powerful elite who influence how we dress, what we buy and how we feel about the faces we see on the screen and the page, in ad campaigns and on album covers. Behind the scenes, costumers like Norris and stylists—who work in advertising and editorial photography—shape the pretty images we often mistake for reality. They are professional shoppers, schleppers and tastemakers, helping their clients look better than they really are, whether by stuffing shoulder pads in the anchorman's jacket or by placing framed family portraits on the politician's desk. They set the tone for the times, and we never even know they're there.

2   If you've ever wondered why movie stars always look so great, the answer is it's no accident. Stylists, wardrobe

Dressing the *thirtysomething* cast (above) has made Norris a confessed "shopaholic". He has flown to Philadelphia where the show is normally set, and to New York City to buy clothes.

supervisors and image consultants get paid anywhere from $150 an hour to $1,200 a day to perfect that high-powered look, onstage and off. When actress Demi Moore appeared in public for the first time after the birth of her baby sporting a whole new wardrobe, it wasn't just a maternal whim, it was the work of stylist Jane Ross, a former Vogue staffer. And when Jodie Foster turns up on TV promoting her latest movie, her classy elegance isn't entirely homegrown. Before the debut of *The Accused,* Foster's mother called celebrity stylist Sharon Simonaire and asked her to please find Jodie something to wear on interviews besides her customary gym clothes.

3   If stylists have one universal complaint, it's that people never really appreciate what it is they do. For Norris, who spends 60 hours a week trying to give the *thirtysomething* characters that label-conscious suburban look, the reward comes from the hundreds of letters he gets from view-

ers who are convinced the actors are actually wearing their own clothes. "I get all these letters asking, 'Where does Nancy buy her sweaters?'" he says. "People are used to fantasy like *Dynasty* and *Dallas.* Because this show is more realistic, they don't think I do anything. But making things look real is much harder."

4   The first thing any stylist or wardrobe supervisor will tell you, is that there is nothing glamorous about their line of work. Even in feature films, the crème de la crème of costuming, it's one hard, grubby job. Gloria Gresham, whose recent films include *When Harry Met Sally...* and *The War of the Roses,* spends weeks before each picture in hot, dusty costume warehouses, often perched on a ladder 12 feet in the air, thumbing through rack after rack of old clothes.

5   In movies, the deadlines are longer and the budgets are bigger, so more of the costumes can be custom-tailored for the stars. Sometimes designing a costume proves easier than finding a dozen backups in the same size and color, which are necessary for any scenes involving stunts. When Charles Grodin was cast at the last minute in the stunt-filled *Midnight Run,* Gresham had to fly from Los Angeles to New York "and spend the weekend searching every corner of the city" to find 12 identical plaid coats.

6   Movie directors aren't the only ones who keep costumers and stylists running full tilt. Sharon Simonaire, who assembles outfits and props for top celebrity photographer Herb Ritts, spends her days and nights scouring Los Angeles for whatever obscure object of desire he requires for his shoots. "Working with Herb, I had to learn to find the most outrageous

things," says Simonaire, who has been Ritts's stylist for the past three years. "He can always visualize it, and I nearly go crazy trying to find it."

7 Simonaire, 33, says she learned all about the power of clothing when she was in sixth grade. Growing up in Baltimore, daughter of a nurse and an engineer, style meant little to her until a doctor's wife she baby-sat for gave her some expensive castoffs—a white minidress and matching go-go boots. "I wore them to school the next day, and as I climbed the steps, every head turned," Simonaire recalls. "It created this allure and mystique. In that moment, I realized the psychological importance of dressing."

8 Graduated from high school at 15, she immediately started working as a clerk in boutiques, later moving on to styling for magazines and fashion ads. As it happens, her latest passion isn't clothes at all: it's home furnishings. In her spare time, Simonaire has opened an antiques-collectibles shop in L.A. called Oddiyana, Tibetan for "beyond imagination."

9 When the final image reaches the public, no one person can take full credit for it. Movies and television are ultimately collaborative efforts, the wardrobe supervisor working closely with the director, producers and actors to create just the right visual cues. Unlike, say, the lighting, on which the technicians are deferred to, when it comes to clothes, everyone has an opinion. "The more contemporary the script, the more people think they know what you should be doing," says Gresham. "I've practically gotten input from the janitor."

10 Nowhere is this more evident than in commercials, where millions of dollars in sales are riding on the ads'

ability to create an irresistible image for the product. Stylists and costumers alike describe advertising work as a "nightmare," and Bill Fucile, a leading commercial stylist, wouldn't disagree. "In a music video, I can say, 'This is what you're all going to wear, because I like it.'" says Fucile, who has styled videos for Tracy Chapman, Rickie Lee Jones and Lou Reed, among others. "In a commercial, you have a lot of people with different ideas and very little time. I have to present five outfits, and the director and ad agency will agree on one. If there are 30 principal players, that's 150 outfits. And I have one week to get them together."

11 For the Levi 501 campaign last year, Fucile worked with 600 pairs of jeans, denim jackets and shirts, ripping, tearing, dyeing, fading and washing them until they conveyed a certain lived-in nonchalance. "Everything in those Levi ads looks real," explains Fucile, "But actually, it's created. Those kids don't just show up in that stuff."

12 Fucile, 31, studied at the Fashion Institute of Design and Merchandising in Los Angeles and at UCLA film school before becoming a stylist. Most of the accounts he works on, including Canada Dry, Sprite and Michelob Dry, are geared toward hip young audiences. "I spend a lot of time people watching," he says, "I go to Melrose Avenue and look at what the kids are wearing on the street. It's amazing how you can show something on TV in an ad and then see it duplicated everywhere a few weeks later."

13 Like most stylists, Fucile is keenly aware of how influential his craft can be. "Television is so powerful," he marvels. "People are so easily influenced by what they see. They don't realize what's going on. It makes you

want to take that power and use it to send kids a message about drug abuse, alcoholism or AIDS, instead of just selling a product."

14   Because stylists spend their days realizing other people's visions, it's particularly important to them that they do something that expresses their own values on their own time. For Norris, that means spending Monday nights at local juvenile-detention halls working with teenagers with drug problems. "It's a commitment that matters to me, given what's going on in society," he says. "The kids are so interested in Hollywood, and I try to show them it can be real. For me, that's as important as anything I get out of this business."

15   Norris and Fucile believe there is a growing interest in the industry in using the tools of their trade to do some good. Fucile and several other stylists have decided to pool their time and talents to work on public-service announcements aimed at young people. "The '80s were so image conscious," Fucile observes. "In the '90s, I think we're going to see more concern for what's behind that image."

● ●

**BUILDING
READING SKILLS**

SCANNING FOR
DETAILS

Scan the article to find the names of several costumers and stylists. Complete the chart by listing the names of these people and their specific jobs.

Name	Job

Answer the following questions.

1. What aspects of our lives do costumers and stylists influence?

   _____

   _____

2. What main complaint do stylists have?

   _____

   _____

3. Why can costumes be more customized in movies?

   _____

   _____

4. Who do costumers and stylists work with to create the final image?

   _____

   _____

5. Why do costumers and stylists think advertising work is so hard?

   _____

   _____

6. Why do most stylists and costumers feel their work is so influential?

   _____

   _____

7. Why do they feel the necessity to express their own vision in their free time?

   _____

   _____

Circle the letter of the choice that best completes each statement.

1. The word *shape* in paragraph 1 is closest in meaning to _____ .

   a. size
   b. form
   c. view
   d. face

2. The phrase *turns up* in paragraph 2 is closest in meaning to _____ .

   a. starts
   b. works
   c. dresses
   d. appears

3. The phrase *thumbing through* in paragraph 4 is closest in meaning to _____ .

   a. examining
   b. handing
   c. cleaning
   d. buying

4. The word *identical* in paragraph 5 is closest in meaning to _____ .

   a. interesting
   b. somewhat similar
   c. medium
   d. exactly alike

5. The word *evident* in paragraph 10 is closest in meaning to _____ .

   a. important
   b. clear
   c. hidden
   d. expensive

6. The word *irresistible* in paragraph 10 is closest in meaning to _____ .

   a. tempting
   b. expensive
   c. sensible
   d. technical

7. The word *conveyed* in paragraph 11 is closest in meaning to _____ .

   a. pleased
   b. communicated
   c. selected
   d. helped

8. The phrase *geared toward* in paragraph 12 is closest in meaning to _____ .

   a. produced by
   b. directed at
   c. contained in
   d. threatened by

9. The word *duplicated* in paragraph 12 is closest in meaning to _____ .

   a. directed
   b. worn
   c. styled
   d. copied

10. The word *pool* in paragraph 15 is closest in meaning to _____ .

    a. combine
    b. use
    c. devote
    d. trust

**BUILDING
WRITING SKILLS**

PARAPHRASING

Rewrite the sentences below using your own words. Your sentence should express the main idea of the original sentence as clearly and simply as possible.

1. *If you've ever wondered why movie stars always look so great, the answer is it's no accident.*

   _____

   _____

2. *If stylists have one universal complaint, it's that people never really appreciate what it is they do.*

   _____

   _____

(continued on the next page)

3. *Unlike, say, the lighting, on which the technicians are deferred to, when it comes to clothes, everyone has an opinion.*

_____

_____

4. *Because stylists spend their days realizing other people's visions, it's particularly important to them that they do something that expresses their own values on their own time.*

_____

_____

TALK IT OVER

DISCUSSION
QUESTIONS

1. Are you influenced by the kinds of hidden persuaders mentioned in this article?

2. Gloria Gresham says that a stylist's job is hard and grubby. What do you think she means by "hard and grubby"? Give some examples.

3. According to the article, in what ways is advertising work a nightmare?

4. How are the 1980s different from the 1990s in terms of stylists' attitudes toward their work?

5. Has your personal style ever been influenced by the way you see people dress on TV or in the movies? What styles can you think of that have become fads this way?

PROVERBS

Read and discuss the following sayings about buying and selling. Think of some more to add to the list.

1. Let the buyer beware.

2. A buyer needs a hundred eyes.

3. The customer is always right.

4. It takes two to make a bargain.

5. The worth of a thing is what someone will pay.

WORD FORMS

A. Complete the chart by filling in the missing forms of the words. The verb forms have been given.

VERB	NOUN	ADJECTIVE	ADVERB
appreciate			
collaborate			
distinguish			
manipulate			
negotiate			
persuade			
promote			
rationalize			
recognize			
signify			

B. Correct the sentences that have errors in word forms.

1. After many years of <u>collaboratively</u>, the authors finally finished the book.

2. My cousin had lost so much weight that I didn't <u>recognition</u> him.

3. Advertisers hope that their campaigns are <u>persuasively</u> enough to attract many buyers.

4. I'm too tired to make a <u>rationalize</u> decision right now.

5. Customers <u>appreciative</u> helpful sales people.

6. The oil industry is of great <u>signify</u> to our economy.

7. After many meetings, the union finally <u>negotiable</u> a new contract with management.

(continued on the next page)

8. It is difficult to work for Kris because she is a very <u>manipulatively</u> manager.

9. It is often difficult to <u>distinguished</u> subtle differences between cultures.

10. The car company's sales <u>promotional</u> was very successful.

C. **Refer to the previous Word Form Charts (pages 22, 48, 74, 104, 139, 165, 188) to answer the following questions.**

1. What suffixes are frequently used to make nouns? List them below and give some examples of each one.

_____   _____

_____   _____

_____   _____

_____   _____

_____   _____

2. What suffixes are used to make adjectives?

_____   _____

_____   _____

_____   _____

_____   _____

_____   _____

_____   _____

3. What suffix is often added to an adjective to make an adverb?

_____   _____

POSTREADING

DISCUSSION
QUESTIONS

1. British author Oscar Wilde once said, "In matters of great importance, style, not sincerity, is the vital thing." Do you agree with him? Why or why not?

2. What do you think makes a successful marketing campaign?

3. There is an old saying, "Don't judge a book by its cover." However, we often judge people and products by their appearances. How can this cause problems?

JUST FOR FUN

TEST YOUR
IMAGE IQ

John Molloy is an image consultant and clothing researcher. He is well-known for his 1961 book called *Dress for Success,* and more recently he has written a sequel called *The New Dress for Success.* As a result, he believes that what we wear affects how we are treated. This is true in business, he says, and it is also true in every other area of our lives. His books are used in many business schools to help people learn to be more effective, confident, and successful.

Take the following quiz[3] and then discuss your answers with your class-mates. Mr. Molloy's answers are on page 230 of the Answer Key.

1. What color raincoat should you wear if you want to appear successful?

2. In which professions only is it OK to wear a bowtie?

3. What tie color makes men look sexy?

4. Should executives wear pants with or without cuffs?

5. Are shirts with a collar of a contrasting color OK to wear in business?

6. If you are going to appear on TV, should you wear stripes or solids?

7. What is the most important sport for you to learn if you want to rise in business?

8. Should a business person carry a pen?

9. Is it OK to wear sunglasses in business?

10. Should a businessman wear ankle-length or over-the-calf socks?

11. In sportswear, what colors should be avoided?

12. What are the best patterns to wear in sportswear?

13. What are the best colors in sportswear?

14. What is the one acceptable sports look that works in all seasons?

15. What kind of shoes should a businessman wear to work?

**READER'S
JOURNAL**

Choose a topic that relates to the readings in this unit and write for about ten to twenty minutes. Consider writing about one of the quotes in this unit or answering one of the discussion questions.

READER'S JOURNAL

Date: _____

_____
_____
_____
_____
_____
_____
_____
_____
_____
_____
_____
_____
_____
_____
_____
_____
_____
_____
_____
_____
_____
_____
_____
_____
_____

| UNIT 1 | JUST FOR FUN | page 24 |

A SHORT HISTORY OF PUNCTUATION

Early Greeks had hardly any punctuation and even changed the direction of their writing at the end of each line. Later they changed to a way of writing that favored right-handed people and showed where a new paragraph began by underlining the first line of it.

Later the Greek playwright Aristophanes invented marks to show where the readers should take a breath.

The Romans made writing much easier to read by putting dots between words and by moving the first letter of a paragraph into the left margin. They adapted some of the Greek marks such as the colon mark to indicate phrase endings.

In the early Middle Ages this system of punctuation broke down because very few people could read and write. But writers kept a space at the end of a sentence and continued to mark paragaphs.

Eventually words were separated again, and new sentences began with a larger letter.

| UNIT 3 | JUST FOR FUN | page 77 |

WORD SCRAMBLE

1. Goya 2. Warhol 3. Vermeer 4. Picasso 5. Rodin 6. Renoir 7. Cassatt 8. El Greco 9. Michelangelo 10. Rembrandt 11. Van Gogh 12. Matisse. *Famous name in the world of art:* Mona Lisa

| UNIT 4 | JUST FOR FUN | page 107 |

CROSSWORD PUZZLE

Across: 1. vital 3. diagnosis 5. Jonas Salk 6. toxic 8. germ 9. herbology 12. acupuncture 15. chronic 16. TCM 17. allopathy 19. longevity 21. wound 22. injure 23. dose
Down: 2. insomniac 4. antibiotic 7. degenerative 10. inject 11. surgeon 13. inheritance 14. immunity 17. ailment 18. robot 20. virus

| UNIT 5 | JUST FOR FUN | pages 140–141 |

TRICKY QUESTIONS

1. You told the driver to let some air out of his tires. This lowers the truck enough to let it through the underpass. Then the driver can stop at the garage ahead and put the air back in his tires. 2. Fill the hole with water from a hose, and the Ping-Pong ball will float to the top. 3. Flapdoodle is bald. 4. 12. 5. The airline clerk had sold the lawyer only one round-trip ticket to Switzerland and also one, one-way ticket. 6. It was still daylight. 7. Throw it up in the air. 8. They make more money cutting the hair of ten men than cutting the hair of one.

| UNIT 6 | JUST FOR FUN | page 167 |

EMOTICONS

1. b 2. k 3. a 4. d 5. m 6. l 7. g 8. c 9. j 10. f 11. e 12. n 13. i 14. h

(continued on the next page)

TOOTHPICK TEASERS

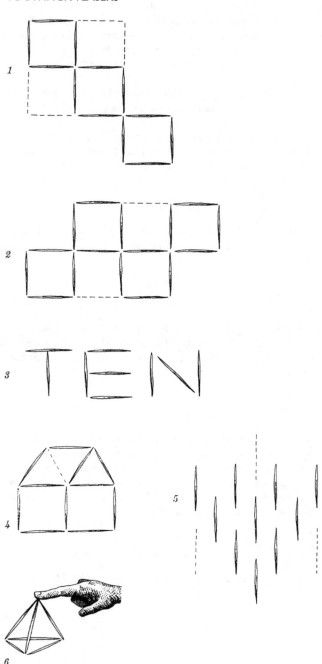

1

2

3

4

5

6

TEST YOUR IMAGE IQ

1. beige 2. college professor, clown, waiter 3. red 4. with cuffs 5. yes 6. solids 7. golf
8. Yes, always. Preferably an expensive one. 9. No, other business people will not trust you. 10. over
the calf 11. light blue, bright yellow 12. Solids and plaids. Avoid dots, stripes, and wild patterns.
13. navy, white, maroon, beige. 14. denim 15. tie shoes

NOTES

Unit 1—Striving to Communicate

1. Davis Wallachinsky and Irving Wallace, *People's Almanac* (Garden City, NY: Doubleday, 1979), p. 749.
2. Extracted from Carl Zimmer, "Early Signifiers," *Discover* (May, 1995): 38–39.
3. Elias Canetti, "1976," *The Secret Heart of the Clock: Notes, Aphorisms, Fragments, 1973–1985* (1991).
4. Gerald Parshall, "A Glorious Mongrel," *U.S. News and World Report* (Sept. 25, 1995): 48.
5. Anthony Burgess, "From Poetry to Slang," *U.S. News and World Report* (Oct. 18, 1993): 73.

Unit 2—Winning Isn't Everything

1. Extracted from William Ecenbarger, "Born to Lose," *Inquirer* (Jan. 29, 1995): 10.

Unit 3—What Is Art?

1. Joshua Fischman, "Painted Puzzles Line the Walls of an Ancient Cave," *Science* (Feb. 3, 1995): 614; Virginia Morell, "Stone Age Menagerie," *Audubon* (May–June, 1995): 55–62.
2. "Stone Age Menagerie," 62.
3. *Art Through the Ages* (New York: Harcourt Brace, 1948) p. 1.

Unit 4—The Marvels of Medicine

1. Microsoft Bookshelf, 1994.
2. Elizabeth DeVita, "The Decline of the Doctor-Patient Relationship," *American Health* (June, 1995) p. 63.
3. Abstracted from Lynn Payer, *Medicine and Culture* (New York: Henry Holt, 1988), p. 265 in Philip R. Cateora, *International Marketing*, 8th ed. (Burr Ridge, IL: Richard D. Irwin, 1993), p. 17.

Unit 5—The Way We Are

1. "What Makes Us Different," *Scholastic Update* (March 12, 1993): 21.

Unit 6—The Age of Information

1. Extracted from "Breaking Point," *Newsweek* (March 6, 1995): 59.
2. "Men, Women and Computers," *Newsweek* (May 16, 1994): 51.
3. Ibid., 54.
4. *Time* (Spring 1995): 62.

Unit 7—The Beauty of Science

1. Carl Sagan in his Introduction to Stephen Hawking, *A Brief History of Time* (New York: Bantam Books, 1988), p. ix.
2. Stephen Hawking, *Black Holes and Baby Universes and Other Essays* (New York: Bantam Books, 1993), p. 29.
3. *World Book Encyclopedia*, 1994 edition, s.v. "black holes."; Noreen Grice, "Black Holes: Powerhouses of the Universe," *Boston Museum of Science Magazine* (April–May, 1995): 10.
4. Farouk El Baz, "Skylab: Next Great Moment in Space," *American Way Magazine* (April, 1973).
5. Carl Sagan in *American Way Magazine* (June, 1978).

Unit 8—The World of Marketing

1. David Ricks, *Blunders in International Business* (Cambridge, MA: Blackwell, 1993): Philip R. Cateora, *International Marketing*, 8th ed. (Burr Ridge, IL: Richard D. Irwin, 1993); Alan M. Rugman and Richard M. Hodgetts, *International Business* (New York: McGraw-Hill, 1995); Pete Engardio et al., "Fast Times on Avenida Madison," *Business Week* (June 6, 1988); G. Christina Hill, "Language for Profit," *Wall Street Journal* (Jan. 13, 1977); E. Jerome McCarthy and William D. Perreault, Jr., *Essentials of Marketing* (Homewood, IL: Irwin, 1991).
2. *Printer's Ink* (February 21, 1964): 53 in Philip R. Cateora, *International Marketing*, 8th ed. (Burr Ridge, IL: Richard D. Irwin, 1993).
3. John T. Molloy, *The New Dress for Success* (New York: Warner Books, 1988).

UNIT 1—Striving to Communicate

The Hope of Esperanto by J.D. Reed. Published in *Time Magazine*, August 3, 1987. © 1987 Time Inc. Reprinted by permission.

Esperanto by Franklin E. Horowitz. From the *Academic American Encyclopedia*, 1995 Edition. Copyright 1995 by Grolier Incorporated. Reprinted by permission.

Reaping the Rewards of Learning English by Jean Caldwell. Published in *The Boston Globe*, May 30, 1994. Reprinted with the permission of Jean Caldwell and courtesy of The Boston Globe.

Half of World's Languages in Danger of Extinction by Daniel Q. Haney. Published in *The Philadelphia Inquirer*, February 19, 1995. Copyright 1995 by The Associated Press. Reprinted by permission.

A Short History of Punctuation by Polly M. Robertus. Published in *Cricket Magazine*, June 1991, Carus Publishing Company. Reprinted with the permission of Polly M. Robertus.

UNIT 2—Winning Isn't Everything

What Winners Know by Pat Riley. Reprinted by permission of the Putnam Publishing Group from *The Winner Within* by Pat Riley. Copyright © 1993 by Riles & Company, Inc.

The Fine Art of Self-Handicapping by Joannie M. Schrof. Published in *U.S. News & World Report*, May 17, 1993. Copyright, May 17, 1993, U.S. News & World Report.

What Makes a Champion by Joe Lewis. Published in *Parade Magazine*, January 29, 1995. Reprinted with permission from Parade, copyright © 1995, and from the author.

"It Couldn't Be Done" by Edgar A. Guest. Reprinted from *The Collected Verse of Edgar Guest* © 1934. Used with permission of Contemporary Books, Inc., Chicago.

UNIT 3—What Is Art?

The Arts Are Essential by Debra Cooper-Solomon. Published in *School Arts*, February 1995. Reprinted with the permission of Debra Cooper-Solomon.

Art Buyers May Not Care If Picasso Was a Monster by Judy Dobrzynski. Reprinted from the July 4, 1988 edition of *Businessweek* by special permission. Copyright 1988 by the McGraw-Hill Companies.

The Many Faces of Picasso. From *Art & Man*, February 1991 issue. Copyright © 1991 by Scholastic, Inc. Reprinted by permission of Scholastic Inc.

They're Stealing Our Masterpieces by Ira Chinoy. Condensed from *Providence Sunday Journal Magazine*, May 20, 1990. © 1990 by The Providence Journal-Bulletin.

UNIT 4—The Marvels of Medicine

Isaac Asimov's Futureworld: Medicine by Isaac Asimov. From *Boys' Life Magazine*, February 1991 issue. By permission of the Estate of Isaac Asimov, c/o Ralph M. Vicinanza, Ltd. and *Boys' Life Magazine*, published by The Boy Scouts of America.

World's First Robot Surgeon Proves a Smooth Operator by Jennifer Pinkerton. Published in *Insight on the News*, June 13, 1994. Reprinted with permission from *Insight*. Copyright 1995 *Insight*. All rights reserved.

The Savior of Summer by Sharon Begley. From *Newsweek*, July 3, 1995. © 1995, Newsweek, Inc. All rights reserved. Reprinted by permission.

Chinese Medicine by Joan Goldstein. Published in *Good Housekeeping*, March 1994 issue. Copyright © 1994 The Hearst Corporation. Reprinted with permission from Good Housekeeping.

Frogs and Human Health by Bill Sharp, in *Sanctuary Magazine*, March/April 1995. Massachusetts Audubon Society. Reprinted by permission.

UNIT 5—The Way We Are

How Color Can Change Your Life by Pamela Stock. Published in *Mademoiselle*, August 1994 issue. Courtesy Mademoiselle. Copyright © 1994 by the Condé Nast Publications Inc.

Smile If You're Feeling Stressed by Brenda Shoss. Published in the National Safety Council's *Safety & Health Magazine*, September 1993 issue. Reprinted with the permission of Brenda Shoss.

Brain Power's Sliding Scale by Judy Foreman. Published in *The Boston Globe*, May 16, 1994. Reprinted courtesy of The Boston Globe.

What Sex Is Your Brain? Adapted from *Brain Sex: The Real Difference Between Men and Women* (pages 50–52) by Anne Moir and David Jessel (Michael Joseph, 1989). Copyright © 1989 Anne Moir and David Jessel. Reproduced by permission of Penguin Books Ltd.

UNIT 6—The Age of Information

TALK to me by Nathan Cobb. Published in *The Boston Globe Magazine*, February 26, 1995. Reprinted courtesy of The Boston Globe.

Gender Gap in Cyberspace by Deborah Tannen. From *Newsweek*, May 16, 1994. © 1994, Newsweek, Inc. All rights reserved. Reprinted by permission.

Cracking Down on Computer Crime by Erik Markus (pen name of Walter Roessing). Published in *Boys' Life Magazine*, March 1993 issue. By permission of Walter Roessing and *Boys' Life Magazine*, published by the Boy Scouts of America.

UNIT 7—The Beauty of Science

Hawking Gets Personal by Michael D. Lemonick. Published in *Time Magazine*, September 27, 1993, p.80. © 1993 Time Inc. Reprinted by permission.

Valuable By-Products of Space Research by David Dooling and Mitchell R. Sharpe. Reprinted from Compton's *Interactive Encyclopedia*, © 1992, 1994, 1995 by Compton NewMedia, Inc. ©1922–1995 Compton's Learning Company. All rights reserved.

Dancing to the Music of Physics. Interview reprinted with the permission of Dr. Steve Huber.

Toothpick Teasers. From *Perplexing Puzzles and Tantalizing Teasers* (pp.24–25, 82–83) by Martin Gardner. Reprinted with the permission of Dover Publications, Inc.

UNIT 8—The World of Marketing

How to Analyze an Ad by Phil Sudo. From *Scholastic Update*, May 7, 1983. Copyright © 1983 by Scholastic Inc. Reprinted by permission of publisher.

Do's and Taboos: Cultural Aspects of International Business by M. Katherine Glover. Published in *Business America*, August 13, 1990, pp.2–6. Reprinted with the permission of Business America.

Style's Hidden Persuaders by Jennet Conant. Published in *People Weekly*, Spring 1990 Special Issue. Reprinted with permission of Jennet Conant and People Weekly. © 1990 Time Inc.